traverse City 44

MW01136826

TORONTO 58

DETROIT 52

Niagara Falls 62

Chicago by Water 16

48

Ann Arbor

Buffalo 66

Cleveland 80

CHICAGO 10

PITTSBURGH 76

the Laurel Highlands 72

Indianapolis 88

Cincinnati 84

The New York Times

36

HOURS

EDITED BY BARBARA IRELAND

The New York Times

HOURS
USA & CANADA

MIDWEST
AND GREAT LAKES

TASCHEN

Contents

Foreword

With cities full of character, country roads leading to unexpected adventures, and eye-openers from glittering art collections to fanatical football, mid-country America is made for weekend trips. Set out in any direction in the great swath of landscape across the Midwestern United States, around the Great Lakes, and into Canada, and the hours from Friday afternoon to Sunday dissolve into a flow of sights, sounds, and surprises. Revived waterfronts and cool updated neighborhoods buzz in towns once dismissed as Rust Belt has-beens. Classic natural destinations from the Black Hills to Niagara Falls flaunt their legendary splendor. People with stories to share pop up everywhere: winemakers along Lake Michigan, conceptual artists in Pittsburgh, cowboys in Valentine, Nebraska.

Choose your weekend and pick your pleasure. Climb around the Ozarks in Arkansas. Measure your height against the length of George Washington's nose at Mount Rushmore. Bike through western Pennsylvania woodlands to whoosh down a natural waterslide. Prefer something more urban? Peer out over St. Louis from its famous Arch or down into Chicago's streets through a scary glass floor 103 stories up. Pay your homage to rock 'n' roll in Cleveland, Motown in Detroit, jazz in Kansas City. Find youthful boutiques and galleries, award-winning chefs, and convivial night spots dotted all over the region.

Care to saturate your senses? Sample chicken wings in Buffalo, cherry ice cream in Traverse City, and microbrews in Milwaukee. Listen for the roar of the Indy 500. Stare at Frank Lloyd Wright's architectural masterpieces scattered over the Midwestern map. Water seems to be everywhere, and it is water that ties this sprawling region together. The Great Lakes connect cities from Toronto to Duluth, and remnants of the old lake-port culture live on in all of them. The other great connector is the Mississippi River, draining the continent from north to south, with its tributaries fingering in every direction and its lore of sternwheelers and rafting explorers reaching out along with them. From Ontario to Oklahoma, a riverside path or a lakefront promenade begs for a lazy stroll in almost every town.

For the traveler, mid-America presents a lot of ground to cover. But a well-plotted itinerary makes all the difference. This book lays out 25 of them, all updated or new, and all adapted from the 36 Hours column in The New York Times, a travel feature that has been inspiring trips and wish lists for more than a decade. Created as a guide to that staple of crammed 21st-century schedules, the weekend getaway, 36 Hours takes readers each week on a carefully researched, uniquely designed two-night excursion to an embraceable place. It charts an experience that identifies the high points of the destination and teases out its character. From the beginning, 36 Hours has been a hit with readers.

In late 2011, The New York Times and TASCHEN published The New York Times 36 Hours: 150 Weekends in the U.S.A. & Canada, which gathered together 150 North American 36 Hours columns in one volume. In 2012, the decision was made to offer this trove of travel guidance in another format: as five regional books, each easily portable and particularly focused, to meet the needs of a traveler who wants to concentrate on one area at a time. You are reading now from one of the five; the others are devoted to the Northeast, the Southeast, the Southwest and Rocky Mountains, and the West Coast including Alaska and Hawaii.

The work of hundreds of writers, photographers, graphic artists, designers, and editors, combining their talents over many years, has gone into 36 Hours and into this book. Each of them shares in its creation. But the star of the story is mid-North America itself, in all of its variety, beauty, and personality.

— BARBARA IRELAND, EDITOR

PAGE 2 Downtown Chicago and Lake Shore Drive, the city's boulevard along Lake Michigan.

PAGE 4 Mississippi River farm country along Highway 52 in Iowa.

OPPOSITE The Gateway Arch in St. Louis symbolizes the city's 19th-century role as an entry point in the great westward migration to the Pacific Coast.

Tips for Using This Book

Plotting the Course: Travelers don't make their way through a region or a country alphabetically, and this book doesn't proceed that way, either. It begins in a major city emblematic of the region and winds from place to place the way a touring adventurer on a car trip might. An alphabetical index appears at the end of the book.

On the Ground: Every *36 Hours* follows a workable numbered itinerary, which is both outlined in the text and shown with corresponding numbers on a detailed destination map. The itinerary is practical: it really is possible to get from one place to the next easily and in the allotted time, although of course many travelers will prefer to take things at their own pace and perhaps take some of their own detours. Astute readers will notice that the "36" in *36 Hours* is elastic, and the traveler's agenda probably will be, too.

The Not So Obvious: The itineraries do not all follow exactly the same pattern. A restaurant for Saturday breakfast may or may not be recommended; after-dinner night life may be included or may not. The destination dictates, and so, to some extent, does the personality of the author who researched and wrote the article. In large cities, where it is impossible to see everything in a weekend, the emphasis is on the less expected discovery over the big, highly promoted attraction that is already well known.

Seasons: The time of year to visit is left up to the traveler, but in general, the big cities are good anytime; towns where snow falls are usually best visited in warm months, unless they are ski destinations; and summer heat is more or less endurable depending on the traveler's own tolerance. The most tourist-oriented areas are often seasonal—some of the sites featured in vacation towns may be closed out of season.

Your Own Agenda: This book is not a conventional guidebook. A *36 Hours* is meant to give a well-informed inside view of each place it covers, a selective summary that lets the traveler get to the heart of things in minimal time. Travelers who have more days to spend may want to use a *36 Hours* as a kind of nugget, supplementing it with the more comprehensive information available on bookstore shelves or on the locally sponsored Internet sites where towns and regions offer exhaustive lists of their attractions. Or, two or three of these itineraries can easily be strung together to make up a longer trip.

Updates: While all the stories in this volume were updated and fact-checked for publication in fall 2011, it is inevitable that some of the featured businesses and destinations will change in time. If you spot any errors in your travels, please feel free to send corrections or updates via email to 36hoursamerica@taschen.com. Please include "36 Hours Correction" and the page number in the subject line of your email to assure that it gets to the right person for future updates.

OPPOSITE The Niagara Falls, viewed from Canada.

THE BASICS	PRICES	Restaurants, dinner without wine:
		Budget, under $15: $
A brief informational box for the	Since hotel and restaurant prices	Moderate, $16 to $24: $$
destination, called "The Basics,"	change quickly, this book uses a	Expensive, $25 to $49: $$$
appears with each *36 Hours* article	system of symbols, based on 2011	Very Expensive, $50 and up: $$$$
in this book. The box provides some	United States dollars.	
orientation on transportation for		Restaurants, full breakfast,
that location, including whether a	**Hotel room, standard double:**	or lunch entree:
traveler arriving by plane should rent	Budget, under $100 per night: $	Budget, under $8: $
a car to follow the itinerary. "The	Moderate, $100 to $199: $$	Moderate, $8 to $14: $$
Basics" also recommends three	Expensive, $200 to $299: $$$	Expensive, $15 to $24: $$$
reliable hotels or other lodgings.	Luxury, $300 and above: $$$$	Very Expensive, $25 and up: $$$$

Chicago

All cities have their ups and downs, but Chicago has learned to play to its strengths, adding parks, architectural crowd pleasers, and public art. A solid base of good urban design and buildings gave the city a lot to build from—this is a place where adventurous architecture was already a tradition, despite the inevitable overlay of urban decay. But now Chicago is going forward, too. A raft of improvements in the last decade or so have left it fortified by both 19th- and 20th-century public spaces brimming with 21st-century attractions. — BY FRED A. BERNSTEIN

FRIDAY

1 *Loop the Loop* 3 p.m.

Even if you've been there in the past, a good place to start in Chicago is at the **Chicago Architecture Foundation** (224 South Michigan Avenue; 312-922-3432; caf.architecture.org). The guided downtown walking tour orients newbies to the late 19th- and early 20th-century buildings that first gave Chicago its reputation as a center of great architecture, and several other walking tours will help give you a feeling for the city. If you already know what to look for, get reacquainted with a ride on the "L," the elevated railway that defines the Loop (transitchicago.com). Get on the brown, orange or pink line—it doesn't matter which color, as long as you sit in the first car by the front-view window—and ride around the two-square-mile area. You'll see Bertrand Goldberg's spectacular **Marina City**, with a design inspired by corncobs; the new **Trump International Hotel and Tower**; Frank Gehry's **Pritzker Pavilion** band shell; and Louis Sullivan's **Auditorium Building**, now part of Roosevelt University.

2 *Midway Fare* 8 p.m.

A number of good midprice but high-style restaurants have opened in Chicago in the past few years. A favorite is **Gilt Bar** (230 West Kinzie Street; 312-464-9544; giltbarchicago.com; $$), a casual restaurant in the River North neighborhood that isn't casual about its cooking. The menu features

OPPOSITE Chicago's urban canyons and the Willis Tower, formerly the Sears Tower.

RIGHT The view down from the Willis Tower Skydeck.

New American dishes like blackened cauliflower with capers and ricotta gnocchi with sage and brown butter. After dinner, head downstairs to **Curio**, a basement bar with a Prohibition theme. Try the Death's Door Daisy, made with artisanal Wisconsin vodka and Aperol, a blood orange liqueur.

3 *Come On In* 11 p.m.

There are so many clubs on Ontario Street, just north of the loop, that it's sometimes known as Red Bull Row. For a mellower jolt, head to the Uptown neighborhood, to **Big Chicks** (5024 North Sheridan Road; 773-728-5511; bigchicks.com) a gay bar that welcomes everyone. The drinks are cheap, the crowd is friendly, and the décor is appealingly kooky.

SATURDAY

4 *Eggs Plus* 9 a.m.

Couldn't get to dinner at Frontera Grill, the nouvelle Mexican restaurant owned by the celebrity chef Rick Bayless? No worries. Just head over to **Xoco** (65 West Illinois Street; 312-661-1434; rickbayless.com; $), another Bayless restaurant. Breakfast is served till 10 a.m.; expect a line after 8:30. Favorites include scrambled egg empanada with poblano chili, and an open-face torta with soft poached egg, salsa, cheese, cilantro, and black beans.

5 *Off-Label Strip* 11 a.m.

The Magnificent Mile area is filled with flagships (Gucci, Vuitton—you know the list). But there are still some independent stores you won't find at your

hometown mall. **Ikram** (873 North Rush Street; 312-587-1000; ikram.com) is the stylish boutique that counts Michelle Obama among its customers, with fashion-forward labels like Jason Wu and Martin Margiela. East Oak Street has a couple of cool shops, including **Sofia** (No. 72; 312-640-0878; sofiavintage.com) and **Colletti Gallery** (No. 102; 312-664-6767; collettigallery.com), with a gorgeous selection of Art Deco and Art Nouveau furniture and

ABOVE The Girl and the Goat, Chef Stephanie Izard's restaurant on Randolph Street just west of downtown.

BELOW Curio, the basement bar beneath Gilt Bar, has a Prohibition theme and a speakeasy atmosphere.

objets. It's a short walk from there to the **Museum of Contemporary Art** (220 East Chicago Avenue; 312-280-2660; mcachicago.org).

6 *First Neighborhood* 2 p.m.

Walking around **Hyde Park**, a leafy enclave about seven miles south of the Loop, it's easy to see why Barack and Michelle Obama settled there. Their house, on South Greenwood Avenue between 50th and 51st Streets, is nearly invisible behind Secret Service barricades. But the streets are great for walking, and the beautifully landscaped **University of Chicago** campus is worth exploring for an afternoon.

7 *Livestock Menu* 7 p.m.

Chicago was once the meatpacking capital of the world, and it still knows what to do with meat. Take **Girl & the Goat** (809 West Randolph Street, 312-492-6262; girlandthegoat.com; $$), a much-blogged-about restaurant where the *Top Chef* winner Stephanie Izard takes livestock parts seriously. The often-updated menu has included the likes of lamb ribs with grilled avocado and pistachio piccata, and braised beef tongue with masa and beef vinaigrette. But you don't have to be a carnivore. If you are vegetarian, there is something for you, too—perhaps chickpeas three ways, and for dessert, potato fritters with lemon poached eggplant and Greek yogurt. The soaring dining room, designed by the Chicago design firm 555 International, is warm and modern, with exposed beams, walls of charred cedar, and a large open kitchen.

8 *Funny Bone* 10 p.m.

You won't find big names at the **Red Bar Comedy Club** (in the Ontourage Night Club, 157 West Ontario Street; 773-387-8412; redbarcomedy.com). But a hit-or-miss roster of itinerant comedians will be looking for laughs, including some who heckle the audience in language that Grandma would not consider polite.

SUNDAY

9 *Beautification Brunch* 10 a.m.

Logan Square, about five to six miles northwest of the Loop, is a remnant of Chicago's late-19th-century beautification movement, with a statue of an eagle by Evelyn Longman where two of the

grandest boulevards meet. Nearby, **Longman & Eagle** (2657 North Kedzie Avenue; 773-276-7110; longmanandeagle.com; $$) is a rough-edged bar that serves a refined brunch featuring items like a chunky sockeye salmon tartare with pickled mango or a wild boar Sloppy Joe.

10 *Grand Piano* 11 a.m.

Chicago knows how to mix neoclassical architecture with contemporary design, and no place in town does it better than the **Art Institute of Chicago** (111 South Michigan Avenue; 312-443-3600; artinstituteofchicago.org), which opened its celebrated Modern Wing in 2009. Designed by Renzo Piano, the luminous addition contains a magnificent set of galleries for 1900-1950 European art (Picasso,

BELOW The Pritzker Pavilion and its Frank Gehry-designed band shell, in Millennium Park.

bikechicago.com) for a ride up the shore of Lake Michigan. You'll pass Navy Pier, skyscrapers by Mies van der Rohe, and hundreds of beach volleyball courts that make this the Malibu of the Midwest on summer and fall weekends. Along the way, you'll see Lincoln Park, with a new pavilion by the Chicago architect Jeanne Gang — another example of how the city is updating its open spaces.

Giacometti, and Klee are among the big names) and a capacious room for the museum's design collection. Hungry or not, check out **Terzo Piano**, the stunning rooftop restaurant with views of the Pritzker Pavilion in Millennium Park across the street.

11 *Wheels Up* 1 p.m.

From the museum, walk over the pedestrian bridge, also designed by Piano, to Millennium Park, and rent bikes from **Bike and Roll** (312-729-1000;

ABOVE Longman & Eagle, a bar that serves a refined brunch, is in the Logan Square neighborhood.

OPPOSITE One way to see great Chicago architecture is to ride the "L," the elevated railway that defines the Loop. Just pay your fare and look out the window.

THE BASICS

Numerous airlines serve Chicago.

Don't try to drive in the city. There's good public transportation.

The Elysian
11 East Walton Street
312-646-1300
elysianhotels.com
$$$$
Cushy 188-room hotel where the beds aren't made — they're "draped" in 460-thread-count Rivolta Carmignani linens.

Hotel Allegro
171 West Randolph Street
312-236-0123
allegrochicago.com
$$
A 483-room hotel in the city's bustling theater district, in the bold style of Kimpton hotels.

The James
55 East Ontario Street
312-337-1000
jameshotels.com
$$$
High-design boutique hotel.

Chicago by Water

Expensive water-view condos and gleaming commercial towers line the Chicago River in downtown Chicago, close to its connection to Lake Michigan. Long ago the river was a polluted dumping ground, but now kayakers ply its waters and tour boats glide along as guides explain some of the wealth of interesting architecture on the banks. For an intimate, easygoing exploration of the river, with stops to look deeper at some of what's close by on land, create your own tour by water taxi. From late spring through fall, two taxi companies operate on the river, running distinct, though partly overlapping, routes. One ventures out into Lake Michigan. The boats operate like buses, following scheduled routes that take you to standard tourist stops. Hop on and off at will, and see the heart of the city from a different point of view.
— BY RUSSELL WORKING

FRIDAY

1 *Know Your River* 3 p.m.

Get your bearings at the **Michigan Avenue Bridge**. Stop on the pedestrian walkway, gaze down the river into the heart of the city and then back the other way toward Lake Michigan. You may spot a water taxi—yellow for Chicago Water Taxi or blue for Shoreline. Inside the ornately decorated stone tower at the southwest corner of the bridge is the **McCormick Tribune Bridgehouse & Chicago River Museum** (376 North Michigan Avenue; bridgehousemuseum.org), where you can see the inner workings of a drawbridge and learn about river history, including the arrival of Jean Baptiste Point du-Sable, a black French pioneer, in the 1780s. At the north end of the bridge, duck down to the lower level and find the **Billy Goat Tavern** (430 North Michigan Avenue; billygoattavern.com), a reporters' watering hole for generations and the inspiration for the *Saturday Night Live* "cheeseburger" sketches with John Belushi as the single-minded counter man.

2 *Down by the Docks* 4 p.m.

Still at the bridge's north end, walk down to water level to see where the taxis leave. For **Chicago Water Taxi** (400 North Michigan Avenue; 312-337-1446; chicagowatertaxi.com for routes and prices), go down the stairs by the **Wrigley Building** and follow the signs to the taxi dock. For **Shoreline Water Taxi** (401 North Michigan Avenue; 312-222-9328; shorelinewatertaxi.com), take the steps down on the northeast side of the bridge. There's no reason to take a water taxi anywhere today, but if you'd like to have the names and histories to go with some of the buildings you'll see on your taxi tour tomorrow, one option is to cross the bridge, walk down the steps on the southern side, and find the dock for the **Chicago Architecture Foundation**'s 90-minute architecture cruise. (To minimize waiting, buy tickets in advance; check caf.architecture.org or go to the foundation's shop at 224 South Michigan Avenue). It's a pleasant, breezy introduction to the heart of the city. Another way to prepare is with a guidebook; a good one is Jennifer Marjorie Bosch's *View From the River: The Chicago Architecture Foundation River Cruise* (Pomegranate Communications).

3 *Mellow Out* 8 p.m.

Relax and plan your strategy for tomorrow over drinks and dinner at **State and Lake** (201 North State Street; 312-239-9400; stateandlakechicago.com; $$), a restaurant that's at least as much about the beverages as the food. The dining choices include comfort food specials, sandwiches and salads, and entrees like steak frites or angel hair pasta and shrimp. Linger over one of the wines or a draft or bottled beer.

SATURDAY

4 *Squint at the Corncobs* 9 a.m.

Return to the Michigan Avenue dock and catch a Chicago Water Taxi headed west. Out on the river, glide along for a while, squinting upward at the skyscrapers in the morning light. There are dozens of landmarks, including the **Marina City** towers at 300 North State Street, designed to resemble corncobs; the sprawling **Merchandise Mart** at North Wells Street, built in 1930; and the **Civic Opera House** on North Wacker Drive, constructed in the Art Deco armchair form and nicknamed Insull's Throne after the tycoon who commissioned it.

OPPOSITE The Merchandise Mart, built in 1930, hulks over the Chicago River, a highway for water taxis.

5 *Waterside* 10 a.m.

Get off at the LaSalle/Clark Street stop and walk across the river on the Clark Street bridge to find the new **Riverwalk** (explorechicago.org). Explore for a while, passing outdoor cafes and kiosks that thrive in the summer season. You're also close here to the area around State and Randolph Streets that is home to several major theaters and the Joffrey Ballet.

6 *Brunch Umbrellas* Noon

A pleasant place for brunch is **Flatwater** (321 North Clark Street, river level; 312-644-0283; flatwater.us; $$), where tables under green umbrellas are lined up close to the river's edge and yachts pull up to dock for lunch. There's also indoor seating, but the river is the real draw here, so why not stay close? (The people watching is good, too.) Check the menu for the crab cakes Benedict. When you're ready to venture out again, return to the LaSalle/Clark Street stop to pick up another taxi and continue west on the river.

7 *Do Look Down* 1:30 p.m.

After the river bends south, alight at the spot near the **Willis Tower** (233 South Wacker Drive; willistower.com), once known as the Sears Tower, where both taxi lines stop. Ride the elevator to the Skydeck (theskydeck.com). Take the dare—venture out onto one of the glass-floored retractable bays to join the other sightseers scaring themselves silly by staring 1,353 feet straight down at the street. Across the river is Union Station, a cavernous rail terminal. Its Beaux-Arts Great Hall has been featured in several films, including *The Untouchables*.

8 *Chinatown* 3:30 p.m.

Continue south on the Chicago Water Taxi to **Ping Tom Memorial Park** (named for a Chinese-American civic leader), and proceed on foot under an ornate gate into **Chinatown**, where you'll find hole-in-the-wall restaurants and stores selling barrels of ginseng or aquariums full of live frogs. Stop in at the one-room **Dr. Sun Yat-Sen Museum** (2245 South Wentworth Avenue, third floor; 312-842-5462; open until 5 p.m.), dedicated to the revolutionary who played a leading role in overthrowing the Qing Dynasty—the last of the Chinese emperors—in 1911. The photos inside include some from Sun's visit to Chicago at around that time. At **Chinatown Square**, an outdoor mall just south of the park, you'll find stores selling green tea and Chinese cookies,

ABOVE The view from the Chicago River up at the Clark Street Bridge.

OPPOSITE ABOVE The Billy Goat Tavern, open since 1934.

OPPOSITE BELOW Aboard the Shoreline Water Taxi.

a Chinese newspaper's offices, and your choice of restaurants. If you'd like an early dinner, try **Spring World** (2109 South China Place in Chinatown Square; 312-326-9966; $), which serves the spicy food of Yunnan Province. When you've seen enough, catch a water taxi for the half-hour trip back to Michigan Avenue.

9 *Honky-Tonk Bard* 7 p.m.

There's enough going on at the **Navy Pier** (navypier.com) to keep you busy all weekend. Reach it from the Michigan Avenue dock of the Shoreline Water Taxi. (And as you debark, take note of the schedule; you don't want to miss the last taxi back.) The pier is 50 acres of parks, promenades, restaurants, carnival-like stalls, and souvenir shops, with fireworks on summer Saturday nights. There's also an indoor garden, a stained-glass museum, and the **Chicago Shakespeare Theater** (800 East Grand Avenue; 312-595-5600; chicagoshakes.com), where you might find local fare in addition to the

serious drama. A few years ago Second City's *Rod Blagojevich Superstar* had a successful run at the theater, including an appearance by Blagojevich himself, although he was still smarting from the scandal that cost him the Illinois governorship. He recited lines from *Henry V* and invited the cast for dinner, adding, "We'll be serving tarantulas."

SUNDAY

10 *Feeding the Spirit* 10 a.m.

From either Michigan Avenue or the LaSalle/Clark stop, it's a short walk to the **House of Blues** (329 North Dearborn Street; 312-923-2000; houseofblues.com; $$$), where the Sunday-morning Gospel Brunch includes a buffet with blackened catfish,

jambalaya, fried chicken, and omelets, along with exhilarating African-American worship and music.

11 *Lakeside Dinosaurs* Noon

For a nice ride out into Lake Michigan, take the Shoreline taxi to the Navy Pier, change boats, and go to the lakeside museum campus that is home to the **Field Museum**, **Shedd Aquarium**, and **Adler Planetarium**. All are worth serious time, but for generations of children, the must-see has

been the Field's dinosaur skeletons, including a Tyrannosaurus rex found in South Dakota in 1990 and nicknamed Sue.

ABOVE The Shedd Aquarium and the Adler Planetarium at Grant Park, on Lake Michigan. Get there from downtown on the Shoreline Water Taxi. Both Shoreline and Chicago Water Taxis cater to commuters and tourists alike.

OPPOSITE Marina City, designed to resemble a corncob.

THE BASICS

The Chicago River, in the heart of downtown, is the north and west boundary of the Loop.

When you're not on a water taxi, take the "L" (that's "El" to some) or land-bound cabs.

Fairmont Chicago Millennium Park
200 North Columbus Drive
312-565-8000
fairmont.com/chicago
$$
Recently renovated; a short walk to the Michigan Avenue bridge.

Wit Hotel
201 North State Street
312-467-0200
thewithotel.com
$$
A chic, fairly new hotel with a popular rooftop bar.

Hotel Sax
333 North Dearborn Street
312-245-0333
hotelsaxchicago.com
$$
Stylish hotel beneath Marina City towers.

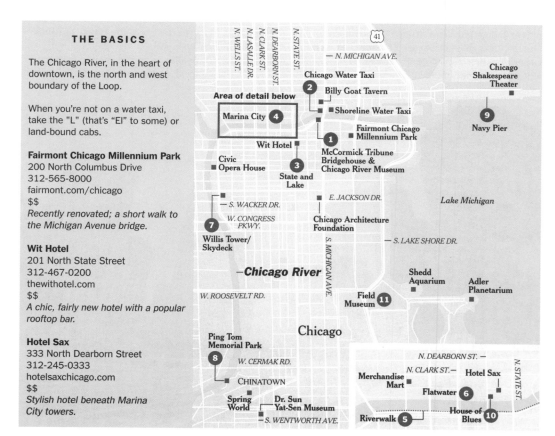

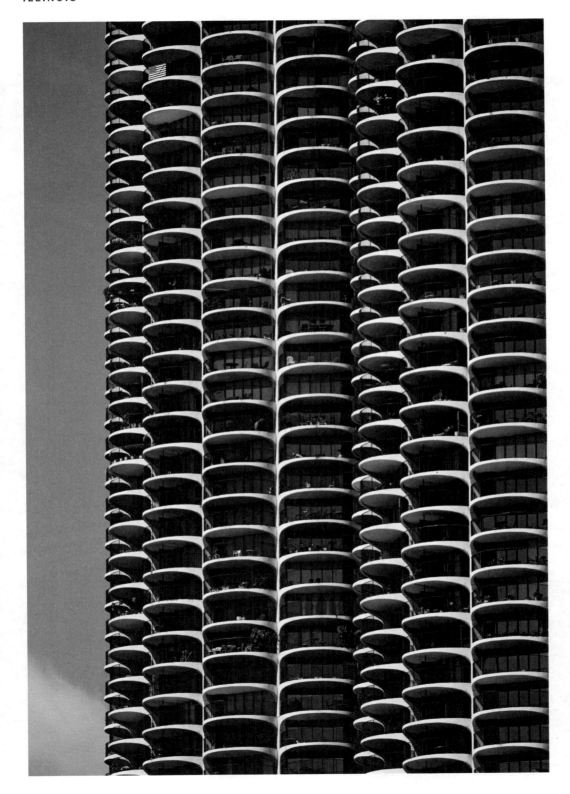

Oak Park

On most weekends, people from all over the world can be seen walking slowly down the streets of Oak Park, Illinois, clutching their maps, guidebooks, audio-tour wands, and cameras. Spotting a celebrity — a house designed by Frank Lloyd Wright — they stop, stare, and snap photographs. Then they move on to the next Wright house amid the historic district's attractive but conventional Victorians. Oak Park, which is the location not only of the home and studio where Wright spent his early career, but of the world's largest collection of his buildings (25), has long attracted design pilgrims. In a weekend there, you will also find galleries, shops, restaurants, and the painstakingly restored childhood home of Ernest Hemingway. And a few miles away in the Hyde Park section of Chicago, another Wright house awaits, one of the master's most renowned.

— BY BETSY RUBINER

FRIDAY

1 *The Son Also Rises* 3 p.m.

Ernest Hemingway was born in Oak Park in 1899 and lived here through high school. Whether Hemingway ever actually described the town as a place of "broad lawns and narrow minds" is in dispute. But you can get a feel for his genteel origins at the **Ernest Hemingway Birthplace Home** (339 North Oak Park Avenue; 708-848-2222; ehfop.org). Just south, at the companion **Ernest Hemingway Museum** (200 North Oak Park Avenue), you can see Hemingway's high school report card (he did well in commercial law, not so well in geometry) and teenage scribblings.

2 *Emerging Artists* 4:30 p.m.

If Oak Park was a good place to create ground-breaking architectural designs and to develop the skills of a landmark novelist, why not for today's generation of creative types? In the **Oak Park Arts District** (Harrison Street between Austin Boulevard and Ridgeland Avenue; oakparkartsdistrict.com), galleries, studios, and shops occupy small store-fronts in a quiet residential neighborhood. Drop in at **Expressions Graphics** (29 Harrison Street; 708-386-3552; expressionsgraphics.org), an artists' cooperative that specializes in prints; at **Prodigy Glassworks** (207 Harrison Street; 708-445-8000;

prodigyglassworks.com), which sells hand-blown and fused glass pieces made by local artists; or at one of the painters' studios. Amid the art spaces are New Age-y offerings like Buddhist meditation, rolfing, and yoga classes.

3 *Carni, Pesce, Paste, Pizze* 6:30 p.m.

Oak Park is a small town, but not too small to have a restaurant with menu headings in Italian. Try out the cuisine at **Mancini's** (1111 Lake Street; 708-445-9700; mancinispizzapastacafe.com; $-$$), an Oak Park fixture since 1976, which serves wine and beer along with its zuppe-to-dolce dinner selections. Don't neglect the gelato.

4 *Reading Up* 8 p.m.

Bone up for a weekend of Frank Lloyd Wright immersion with some selections from the **Book Table** (1045 Lake Street; 708-386-9800; booktable.net), which stocks several titles on the master in its pleasant, book-filled store. Wright's profoundly original and seminal architecture is what assures his continuing fame, but when he was alive, his flamboyant personality garnered more attention. As you pick up some books of your own, you can go serious, with scholarly architectural criticism; local, focusing on Wright in Oak Park; or gossipy, digging into recent books on the architect's sometimes messy, sometimes tragic private life.

OPPOSITE AND BELOW The sanctuary of Unity Temple and the exterior of the Frank Lloyd Wright Home and Studio. Wright designed both structures, and several others in town, during his years as an Oak Park resident.

SATURDAY

5 *The Main Attraction* 10:30 a.m.

Before Frank Lloyd Wright built homes for clients, he field-tested many of his design principles in the house he built for his first wife and their six children. Wright built a compact dark-wood and light-brick New England Shingle-style home in 1889, and in 1898 he added the eye-catching studio addition where he developed his Prairie style. Walking through his rooms during the guided interior tour of what is now the **Frank Lloyd Wright Home and Studio** (951 Chicago Avenue; 708-848-1976; gowright.org), you experience his ideas about space, light, and shelter. You'll also see his signature touches — the art glass, the central hearth, the intimate spaces tucked within the open plan. During a guided walking tour (exteriors only) of other Wright-designed homes nearby, you'll see how his ideas evolved. Arrive early or buy advance tickets online — tours often fill quickly.

6 *On the Avenue* 1:30 p.m.

For over a century, the intersection of Oak Park Avenue and Lake Street has been a lively retail area known by locals as "the Avenue." Stop for lunch at **Winberie's** (151 North Oak Park Avenue; 708-386-2600; winberies.com; $$) in a 1905 Prairie-style commercial building in Scoville Square. It's a bistro with large picture windows, exposed brick walls, and shiny white-and-black tile floors, and it serves a broad selection of sandwiches, salads, and pastas.

7 *The Jewel Box* 3 p.m.

Sitting sternly, almost bunkerlike, on a busy downtown street, **Unity Temple** (875 Lake Street; 708-383-8873; unitytemple.org) is one of Wright's most

influential buildings and is still home to its original Unitarian Universalist congregation. The building resembles three giant children's blocks made of poured concrete. A guided tour leads you through a low, dark cloister and into a stunning high-ceilinged sanctuary filled with light filtered through art-glass windows. The intimate, minutely detailed interior is profoundly calming. Wright called it his "little jewel box."

8 *Try the Thai* 7 p.m.

Rangsan Sutcharit, who once cooked at Arun's, a superb Thai restaurant in Chicago, now cooks simpler and less expensive but still delicious Thai food, combining fresh ingredients and pungent spices, at **Amarind's** (6822 West North Avenue, Chicago; 773-889-9999; amarinds.com; $). It's in a small brick castle-like building on an easy-to-miss corner just over Oak Park's northern border with Chicago. Don't miss the Golden Cup appetizer, delicate flower-shaped pastry cups filled with corn, shrimp, sweet peas, and shiitake mushrooms. The signature entree is spinach noodles with shrimp and crab in a chili sauce.

9 *Roots Music* 9:30 p.m.

A weathered club inside a green wood-frame building, **FitzGerald's** (6615 West Roosevelt Road, Berwyn; 708-788-2118; fitzgeraldsnightclub.com) still looks and feels like a 1920s roadhouse. But it sits back slightly on a commercial strip in Berwyn, just south of Oak Park. One of the best places in the Chicago area to hear live roots music, FitzGerald's has long been host to impressive national and local musicians who play everything from Chicago blues to R&B, jazz, rock, and alternative country. Bands play on a simple raised

ABOVE Frank Lloyd Wright is Oak Park's main claim to fame, but Ernest Hemingway spent time there, too — from birth through high school. His home is open for tour.

RIGHT Spring in an Oak Park city park.

stage for a beer-in-hand crowd gathered on the scuffed wooden dance floor.

SUNDAY

10 *Going Organic* 9 a.m.

The buzz about **Buzz Café** (905 South Lombard Avenue; 708-524-2899; thebuzzcafe.com; $) is that it's a community-minded gathering spot, with plenty of organic and vegetarian choices, in the Harrison Street Arts District. Paintings and drawings by local artists cover the green and purple walls, artists sketch at tables while sitting on brightly painted second-hand chairs, and children and reading groups curl up on comfy sofas in the back. Sunday brunch entrees includes eggs and sausage, pancakes, waffles, and wraps.

11 *Chicago Prairie* 11 a.m.

Wright's Oak Park houses show the development of his style in his first decades as an architect, culminating in his signature Prairie houses. To see the Prairie house in full flower and on a scale that only his wealthiest clients could afford, journey to the Hyde Park neighborhood of Chicago to tour his **Robie House** (5757 South Woodlawn Avenue, Chicago; 312-994-4000; gowright.org). This is a masterpiece, one of the clearest examples anywhere of a building that is fully, from top to bottom and inside and out, an integrated and harmonious work of art.

THE BASICS

Oak Park is a 20-minute drive or train ride from downtown Chicago.

The Chicago area is well served by public transportation.

Carleton of Oak Park
1110 Pleasant Street
708-848-5000
carletonhotel.com
$$
Dated but in a perfect location, with 153 rooms in two buildings.

Harvey House Bed & Breakfast
107 South Scoville Avenue
708-848-6810
harveyhousebb.com
$$$
Five nicely appointed rooms; massage available.

Under the Ginkgo Tree Bed and Breakfast
300 North Kenilworth Avenue
708-524-2327
undertheginkgotreebb.com
$
Four pleasant rooms in a Queen Anne Victorian.

Milwaukee

There's plenty about modern-day Milwaukee, Wisconsin, that would be unrecognizable to Laverne and Shirley from the sitcom set in the late '50s and '60s. Oh, the area still appreciates its beer and bratwurst: delis carry a mind-boggling variety of sausage, and bars are known to have 50-plus brands of brew. But Milwaukee also has 95 miles of bike lanes, lush parks lacing the shores of Lake Michigan, and a revitalized riverfront where sophisticated shops coexist within sight of the city's industrial past. Modern Milwaukee is defined less by the Rust Belt than by its lively downtown and a signature museum so architecturally striking that it competes for attention with the art it holds. — MAURA J. CASEY

FRIDAY

1 *Hog Heaven* 4 p.m.

Roar on over to the **Harley-Davidson Museum** (400 Canal Street; 877-436-8738; h-dmuseum.com), which celebrates the 1903 birth of the signature product of Milwaukee residents William Harley and Arthur Davidson, and the American icon it has become. The Harley-Davidson Museum has 138 motorcycles on display, including the company's first two models, from 1903 and 1905, a 1920 Sport model marketed to women, and the 1932 Servi-Car used for commercial deliveries and credited with keeping the company solvent during the Great Depression. Harley-Davidson has been setting aside at least one motorcycle every year since 1915, and the resulting collection tells the story of a machine, America, and the open road in the 20th century—an absorbing tale whether or not you ride.

2 *Snake Chasers* 6 p.m.

There's more to Milwaukee than beer, but beer undeniably helped build the city. At one point in the 19th century, 150 breweries flourished here, some established by German immigrants whose names were Pabst, Miller, and Schlitz. So to better appreciate all that history and perhaps take a sip yourself, tour the **Lakefront Brewery** (1872 North Commerce Street;

OPPOSITE Inside the Quadracci Pavilion, designed by Santiago Calatrava, at the Milwaukee Art Museum.

RIGHT Lake Michigan and the Milwaukee skyline.

414-372-8800; lakefrontbrewery.com), housed in a century-old former utility building with soaring, 30-foot-high ceilings. You'll learn about how beer is made and taste a few of Lakefront's winning brews, including the Snake Chaser, an Irish-style stout made in honor of St. Patrick's Day. The guides are very funny, so for the laughs alone, it's worth the trip.

3 *Slavic Feast* 8 p.m.

For authentic Eastern European flavors, you can't do better than **Three Brothers Bar and Restaurant** (2414 South St. Clair Street; 414-481-7530; 3brothersrestaurant.com; $$), a Milwaukee institution that has been serving Serbian cuisine since 1954. Where else could you order roast suckling pig with rice and vegetables, served with home-pickled cabbage? Or a chicken paprikash followed by an incredibly light seven-layer walnut torte? The dining room has the unpretentious feel of a neighborhood tavern.

SATURDAY

4 *A Ward Updated* 10 a.m.

Many cities have warehouse districts that have become revitalized; Milwaukee has the **Historic Third Ward** (historicthirdward.org), made up of the blocks between the Milwaukee River and Jackson Street. A century ago, this was a manufacturing center. Now it is a magnet for shoppers, with old brick warehouses converted into boutiques and restaurants. For distinctive fashions, search no farther than **Five Hearts Boutique** (153 North Milwaukee Street;

414-727-4622; shopfivehearts.com). And for an eclectic and international array of home furnishings and artifacts, linger in **Embelezar** (241 North Broadway; 414-224-7644), whose name is Portuguese for, fittingly enough, "to embellish and adorn."

5 *Sausage and Cheese* Noon

Before finding a spot to hang out in one of the city's lovely waterfront parks, pack a picnic on Old World Third Street, the center of German life in 19th-century Milwaukee. The **Wisconsin Cheese Mart** (215 West Highland Avenue; 888-482-7700; wisconsincheesemart.com), which opened in 1938, sells hundreds of varieties of cheese. A few doors down is **Usingers** (1030 North Old World Third

Street; 800-558-9998; usinger.com), sausage makers since 1880. There are 70 varieties, including a lean summer sausage.

6 *Spreading Wings* 1:30 p.m.

The **Milwaukee Art Museum** (700 North Art Museum Drive; 414-224-3200; mam.org) may have opened in 1888, but the eye-catching Quadracci Pavilion, designed by Santiago Calatrava and opened in 2001, has become a symbol of modern Milwaukee. With its movable wings expanded to their full, 217-foot span, the building looks either like a large white bird landing on Lake Michigan or the tail of a white whale emerging from the water. There's art, too: extensive collections of folk, central European and Germanic, and post-1960 contemporary.

7 *Find Your Title* 4 p.m.

The first floor of the **Renaissance Book Shop** (834 North Plankinton Avenue; 414-271-6850), in a century-old former furniture store, looks like a book collector's attic, with boxes of used books lining the floor. But it's more organized than it looks, with about half a million books parceled among dozens of categories (Animal Husbandry, Theater Practices and Problems) spread across three floors and a basement. When you're finished shopping, move on to the west side of the Wells Street Bridge for a look at the Bronzie Fonzie, a life-size statue of the Fonz, the iconic television character from *Happy Days.* It's a favorite spot for a photograph, so smile and remember: two thumbs up for the camera.

8 *Popover Delight* 7 p.m.

If you need to give your arteries a rest, try some lighter fare at **Coast** (931 East Wisconsin Avenue; 414-727-5555; coastrestaurant.com; $$$), an elegant fish and seafood restaurant. Look for baked local walleye served on a cedar plank with roasted red potatoes and haricots verts. The warm popovers are to die for. If you are ready to throw your cholesterol numbers to the wind, try a dessert, perhaps the Praline Pyramid: layers of pecans, meringue wafers, Grand Marnier butter cream, and chocolate ganache glaze.

9 *Blues in the Night* 9:30 p.m.

East Brady Street, which stretches for about eight blocks from Lake Michigan to the Milwaukee River, was a hippie hangout in the 1960s. Today, its well-preserved buildings and 19th-century Victorian homes are a backdrop to one of the city's liveliest neighborhoods. During the day, boutiques and small stores draw shoppers. At night, restaurants and bars keep the street lively. A good spot for music is the **Up and Under Pub** (1216 East Brady Street; 414-276-2677; theupandunderpub.com), which proclaims itself the blues capital of Milwaukee. With high ceilings, an antique bar and a couple of dozen beers on tap, it offers live blues, rock, and reggae until 2 a.m. There's usually a $5 cover. If you'd rather avoid alcohol, **Rochambo Coffee and Tea House** down the street (1317 East Brady Street; 414-291-0095; rochambo.com) offers dozens of teas and stays open until midnight.

OPPOSITE ABOVE The Harley-Davidson Museum.

OPPOSITE BELOW Up and Under Pub, a home of the blues.

BELOW Updated tradition at the Lakefront Brewery.

SUNDAY

10 *Lakeside Brunch* 10 a.m.

The Knick (1030 East Juneau Avenue; 414-272-0011; theknickrestaurant.com; $$) is busy and breezy on Sunday mornings, with an outdoor patio near Lake Michigan overlooking Veterans Park. For a memorable breakfast, try the crab hash, a mixture of crabmeat, onions, and hash browns topped with two eggs, or the banana pecan pancakes, dripping with whiskey butter and served with maple syrup.

11 *Wisconsin Tropics* 1 p.m.

Rain or shine, the **Mitchell Park Horticultural Conservatory** (524 South Layton Boulevard; 414-649-9830; countyparks.com) offers perennial respite. Affectionately known as the Domes, the conservatory is housed in three 85-foot-high, beehive-shaped buildings with different climates: the Floral Dome has more than 150 floral displays; the Arid Dome mimics the desert, with an oasis-like pool surrounded by cactuses; and the Tropical Dome has 1,200 rain-forest plants, tropical birds flying overhead and a 30-foot waterfall.

ABOVE Choose a cheese at Wisconsin Cheese Mart.

OPPOSITE Green space along the waterfront.

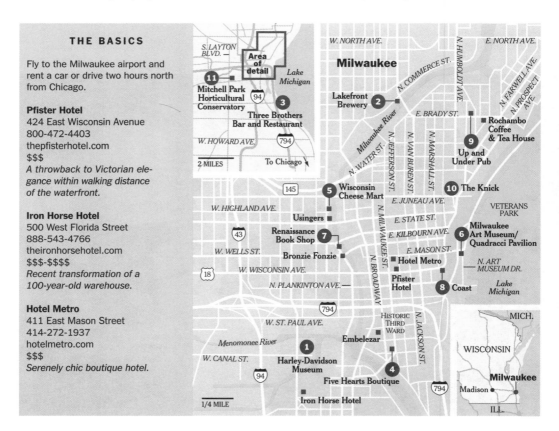

THE BASICS

Fly to the Milwaukee airport and rent a car or drive two hours north from Chicago.

Pfister Hotel
424 East Wisconsin Avenue
800-472-4403
thepfisterhotel.com
$$$
A throwback to Victorian elegance within walking distance of the waterfront.

Iron Horse Hotel
500 West Florida Street
888-543-4766
theironhorsehotel.com
$$$-$$$$
Recent transformation of a 100-year-old warehouse.

Hotel Metro
411 East Mason Street
414-272-1937
hotelmetro.com
$$$
Serenely chic boutique hotel.

Madison

Madison, Wisconsin, a liberal college town that doubles as the capital of a politically complicated state, pulls its disparate elements together into a spirited reality all its own, a funky amalgam of hard-partying students, socially conscious activists, sports fans, outdoor warriors, politicos from both sides of the aisle, artists, foodies, and more. Long pigeonholed as a hotbed for frat parties and activism, Madison has a vibrant but much more tempered side brimming with arts, culture, and food. In a city with so many types to keep happy, it's impossible not to find something that suits your fancy. — BY KATIE ZEZIMA

FRIDAY

1 *Glimpse of Gridiron* 3 p.m.

University of Wisconsin football inspires obsession, drawing pilgrims even in the off-season to **Camp Randall Stadium** (1440 Monroe Street; 608-263-5645; uwbadgers.com/facilities). Groups of 10 to 75 can reserve free tours that take them onto the field and inside locker rooms and luxury boxes. If you can't find nine friends to go along, you may be able to latch on with a scheduled group; in either case, you must call at least two weeks in advance. Otherwise, peek at the field from a window in the apparel store at the stadium, **Bucky's Locker Room** (inside Gate 1; 608-256-9499), while you're picking up your Badgers cap. Or forget football and explore the **Allen Centennial Gardens** (620 Babcock Drive; allencentennialgardens.org), 2.5 acres of flowers and plants from daylily-lined path to a French garden with shrubs trimmed in the shape of fleurs-de-lis.

2 *Beer and Water* 6 p.m.

Drink in views of Lake Mendota, one of the lakes that give Madison its miles of waterfront, along with your pint at the **Memorial Union Terrace** at the **University of Wisconsin** (800 Langdon Street; 608-265-3000; union.wisc.edu/terrace), an outdoor four-tiered space with candy-colored chairs, a lakefront path, and live music in the warm months.

3 *Prairie Provisions* 8 p.m.

Madison's culinary scene pulls diners in two very different directions: far from the prairie with dozens of ethnic restaurants and right back to it with an emphasis on the bounty of Wisconsin farms. Expect to see Wisconsin grass-fed beef and house-made pasta on the menu at **Harvest** (21 North Pinckney Street; 608-255-6075; harvest-restaurant.com; $$$). It offers sophisticated seasonal dishes and an extensive wine list in a soothing setting of soft lighting and buttery yellow walls.

SATURDAY

4 *Biking among Badgers* 9 a.m.

Centered on an isthmus between Lakes Mendota and Monona and surrounded by conservation land, Madison is a haven for outdoors types and one of the most bicycle-friendly cities in the country. For some easy exploring, join the biking crowd by picking up a rental at **Machinery Row Bicycles** (601 Williamson Street; 608-442-5974; machineryrowbicycles.com), which sits on the bike path around Monona. Ride around the lake or head over to the 1,260-acre **University of Wisconsin Arboretum** (1207 Seminole Highway; 608-263-7888; uwarboretum.org).

OPPOSITE Badgers loyalists during a football game at the University of Wisconsin in Madison.

RIGHT Late afternoon at Memorial Union Terrace on the University of Wisconsin campus.

5 *The Architect* 1 p.m.

These days Wisconsin wants you to know it was the first and favorite home of Frank Lloyd Wright, but in his lifetime it wasn't so sure. Wright's vision for a sprawling lakeside civic center was rejected in 1938 by one planning-commission vote. In the 1990s, the design was resurrected and Madison built **Monona Terrace** (1 John Nolen Drive; 608-261-4000; mononaterrace.com; tours daily at 1 p.m.). Its open design and tinted windows reflect the water below, and its roof garden and cafe offer the city's best water view. One group that did appreciate Wright was the congregation that hired him to design the **Unitarian Meeting House** (900 University Bay Drive; 608-233-9774; fusmadison.org), completed in 1951. Take a formal tour or look from outside. The church's bold design is unmistakable Wright. The building is a triangle, symbolizing hands clasped in prayer.

6 *Make Mine Cheesy* 3 p.m.

The Old Fashioned (23 North Pinckney Street; 608-310-4545; theoldfashioned.com) serves the food that "makes Wisconsin so Wisconsin," so it's no surprise that an entire section of the menu is devoted to cheese. The bar and restaurant is reminiscent of a late-19th-century saloon filled with Grandma's antiques, but with an updated flair. The cheese curds are a must for sampling, as is the spicy bloody mary.

7 *Where the Shoppers Are* 4 p.m.

Stroll State Street, which links the Capitol with the university. It's a pedestrian thoroughfare brimming with boutiques, restaurants, museums, and bars. Check out **Anthology** (No. 218; 608-204-2644; anthology.typepad.com), a whimsical boutique filled with colorful crafts; the **Soap Opera** (No. 319; 800-251-7627; thesoapopera.com), a fragrant repository of soaps, lotions, and potions; and **B-Side**

Records (No. 436; 608-255-1977; b-sidemadison.com), a trove of vintage vinyl and CDs and a showcase for many of the city's bands.

8 *Andes Express* 8 p.m.

Inka Heritage (602 South Park Street; 608-310-4282; inkaheritagerestaurant.com; $$) is one of Madison's culinary bright spots, and not just because of its fluorescent walls and lively art. Diners are transported to Peru via dishes like fire-roasted beef heart, grilled Peruvian trout, and fried yucca. The wine list includes several selections from Chile and Argentina.

9 *Swing Time* 10:30 p.m.

Madison is a late-night kind of town, especially for fans of live music. Check out a show at the **High Noon Saloon** (701A East Washington Avenue; 608-268-1122; high-noon.com), a large, Western-tinged club with a balcony for catbird views of bands. The club is operated by the former owner of Madison's once beloved O'Cayz Corral, which was destroyed by fire in 2001.

SUNDAY

10 *Double Comfort Score* 10 a.m.

Any restaurant that spells out its name in large Scrabble tiles near the front door is bound to have a

RIGHT B-Side Records, one of the shopping options on State Street, which links the university and the State Capitol.

funky-nerdy-vibe. **Lazy Jane's Cafe and Bakery** (1358 Williamson Street; 608-257-5263; $) becomes crowded and loud but exudes the coziness that comes with a lazy Sunday poring over the newspaper or catching up with an old friend. The food is similarly comfortable, with scones, frittata, grilled cheese sandwiches, and a seitan scramble filled with peppers, onions, and mushrooms that is good enough to impress an avowed meat eater.

11 *Easy Paddling* 11:30 a.m.

Lakes Monona and Mendota are usually the first choices for fun on the water in Madison, but tiny **Lake Wingra**, tucked south of the university arboretum and the Henry Vilas Zoo, is a quieter option. Rent a canoe,

kayak, rowboat, or paddle boat at **Wingra Boats** (824 Knickerbocker Street; 608-233-5332; wingraboats.com), and glide away.

OPPOSITE ABOVE A tour group in Camp Randall Stadium.

ABOVE The Old Fashioned, where the furniture suggests a raid on Grandma's parlor, serves the food that "makes Wisconsin so Wisconsin." Try the cheese curds.

THE BASICS

Drive three hours from Chicago or fly into Dane County Airport and rent a car.

Doubletree Madison
525 West Johnson Street
608-251-5511
doubletreemadison.com
$$
Between the university and Capitol Square; offers airport shuttle service.

Dahlmann Campus Inn
601 Langdon Street
608-257-4391
thecampusinn.com
$$
A touch of boutique refinement in the heart of the campus

Arbor House
3402 Monroe Street
608-238-2981
arbor-house.com
$$
Proudly green, with a native-plant garden and an environmental resource center.

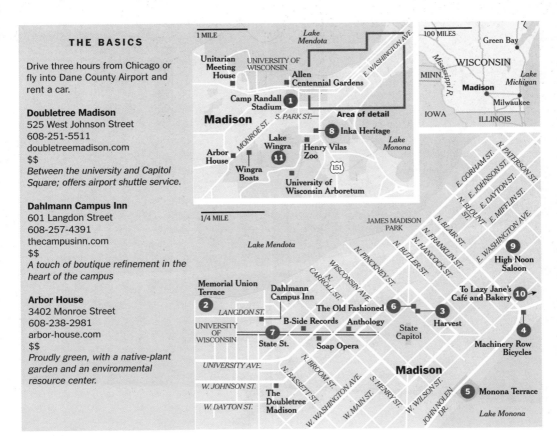

Minneapolis-
St. Paul

Minnesotans take pride in their humility, but make an exception when it comes to showing folks around. And they have a lot to show. There is a depth of cultural amenities to Minneapolis and its not-so-twin city St. Paul that will surprise a first-time visitor. And please remember, when they ask you at the coffee shop, "How you doing, today?" they really want to know.
— BY DAVID CARR

FRIDAY

1 *By the Falls of Minnehaha* 5 p.m.

On a hot summer day, there is convenient and diverting respite at **Minnehaha Falls Park** (4825 Minnehaha Avenue South; 612-230-6400; minneapolisparks.org). Don't go there expecting Niagara; rather, you'll find a quaint urban park with both landscaped and wild elements, a surprisingly good seafood restaurant (Sea Salt Eatery) and, of course, the 53-foot falls that inspired Henry Wadsworth Longfellow to write *The Song of Hiawatha*. Now, Longfellow never actually saw the falls — he was inspired by the writing of others — but why put such a fine point on it?

2 *Intermission with a View* 7 p.m.

Many cities in the middle of the country chirp reflexively about their "great theater," but Minneapolis lives up to its rhetoric with strong independent companies. Among them is the **Guthrie Theater** (818 South Second Street; 612-377-2224; guthrietheater.org), a first-rate repertory theater with a new facility featuring a cantilevered bridge to nowhere. Step out and you can see all the way to the city's industrial northeast. Inside, you can take in a well-acted play.

3 *To the Warehouses* 8 p.m.

People are of two minds about Minneapolis's warehouse district. There are those who live for the street-filling frolic of a Friday night, and many who would drive miles to avoid it. A point for the former is the **112 Eatery** (112 North Third Street; 612-343-7696; 112eatery.com; $$), where you can avoid the mob by going to the upstairs bar for the tagliatelle with foie gras meatballs. Afterward, liquid diversions can commence. Start at the **Monte Carlo** (219 Third Avenue North; 612-333-5900). Lawyers, politicos, and media types congregate here amid a mind-boggling, and potentially mind-bending, array of alcohol. Move on to **Lee's Liquor Lounge** (101 Glenwood Avenue; 612-338-9491; leesliquorlounge.com), just west of downtown, where Trailer Trash may be playing. You can face-plant at the nearby and artful Chambers hotel, or just have a nightcap on the rooftop then cab back to your own hotel.

SATURDAY

4 *You Going to Eat That?* 10 a.m.

Tell room service to keep it quiet when they deliver coffee. Or if you are feeling ambitious, go to **Al's Breakfast** in Dinkytown (413 14th Avenue Southeast; 612-331-9991), hard by the east-bank campus of the University of Minnesota. Wait against the wall for one of 14 stools while eyeing the food of the patron whose stool you are coveting. Minnesota is a friendly place, but don't ask for a bite of his blueberry pancakes. Order the hash browns and forswear ever eating so-called home fries again.

OPPOSITE The Guthrie Theater in Minneapolis.

RIGHT Claes Oldenburg and Coosje van Bruggen's giant sculpture called *Spoonbridge and Cherry* sits in the center of the Walker Art Center's sculpture garden in Minneapolis.

5 *Necklace of Blue* 11:30 a.m.

So many lakes right in the city, but which one is for you? If you wear socks with sandals and think walking is a sport, **Lake Harriet** is for you. If you are prone to nudity and like swimming at night, then it's Hidden Beach at Cedar Lake. The rest of us can go to **Lake Calhoun**. Wheels of any kind, most commonly rollerblades, take you around it, but why not go to the boathouse and get a canoe? Avoid the sailboats and windsurfers by paddling under the bridge into Lake of the Isles, which is sort of swampy to walk around, but lovely from the water.

6 *Spoon Feeding* 2:30 p.m.

The **Walker Art Center** (1750 Hennepin Avenue; 612-375-7600; walkerart.org) has one of the best contemporary art collections between the coasts, but why not stay outside for a little artist-designed mini-golf? At the sculpture garden, one might be tempted to climb into the giant spoon by Claes Oldenburg and Coosje van Bruggen. Don't. Motion detectors were installed after locals decided to memorialize their love with nocturnal visits. **Café Lurcat** (1624 Harmon Place; 612-486-5500; cafelurcat.com; $$), across the walking bridge, has excellent small plates.

7 *Ambulatory Retail* 4:30 p.m.

Shopping in Minnesota is usually reductively assigned to the Mall of America, but there is a strollable necklace of stores along Grand Avenue in St. Paul where down-home and style make nice. **Bibelot** (No. 1082; 651-222-0321; bibelotshops.com) has been featuring cool local stuff for four decades, and **Cooks of Crocus Hill** (No. 877; 651-228-1333;

cooksofcrocushill.com) is the foodie perennial that just won't quit. If you get hungry or thirsty, you can always walk in to **Dixie's on Grand** (No. 695; 651-222-7345; dixiesongrand.com) for some Southern-inspired fare.

8 *The North Star* 7 p.m.

As in many urban areas, the ineffable epicenter of cool migrates on a schedule known only to a select few. In Minneapolis, the indigenous tribe of artists, musicians, and wannabes have forsaken Uptown for Northeast, where trendy restaurants and bars have taken root. **Brasa Rotisserie** (600 East Hennepin Avenue; 612-379-3030; brasa.us) is a new-ish favorite where precious food localism comes without a dear price. Another is **331 Club** (331 13th Avenue Northeast; 612-331-1746; 331club.com), with a neighborhood vibe even a visitor can't miss. Yes, you should try the Hot Polack, a mix of jalapeños, kraut, and bratwurst. And anyone who knows Minneapolis will ask if you visited **Nye's Polonaise Room** (112 East Hennepin Avenue; 612-379-2021; nyespolonaise.com) to sample its wondrously cheesy piano bar and slamming polka.

9 *Here Comes a Regular* 11 p.m.

The Replacements may not drink anymore at the **CC Club** (2600 Lyndale Avenue South; 612-874-7226;

ABOVE Cooks of Crocus Hill on Grand Avenue in St. Paul.

RIGHT 20.21, a Wolfgang Puck restaurant inside the Walker Art Center in downtown Minneapolis.

OPPOSITE You can walk or bike at Lake Calhoun, but why not go to the boathouse and get a canoe?

myspace.com/theccclub). And Tom Arnold was 86'ed for the last time a while ago. But the venerable club remains a nexus for the city's down and dirty rock scene. Plus, there's a killer juke box and no live music to try to talk over.

SUNDAY

10 *Over the River* 9 a.m.

Head over the river and check out St. Paul's **City Hall** (15 Kellogg Boulevard West; stpaul.gov), where *Vision of Peace*, a 60-ton onyx statue, towers over a lobby done in black Zigzag Moderne. And try to grab a booth at **Mickey's Diner** (36 Seventh Street West; 651-222-5633; mickeysdiningcar.com).

11 *A Historic Visit* Noon

Historic museums in fairly young places like Minnesota can be dreary, but not so at the **Minnesota History Center** (345 Kellogg Boulevard West, St. Paul; 651-259-3000; mnhs.org/historycenter). Get some metaphorical manure on your boots by visiting the Grainland/Boxcar exhibit. After all the eating you've done, it's worth finding out what happens inside those big elevators that tower over middle America. The hokey charms of so-called Minnesota Nice loom large.

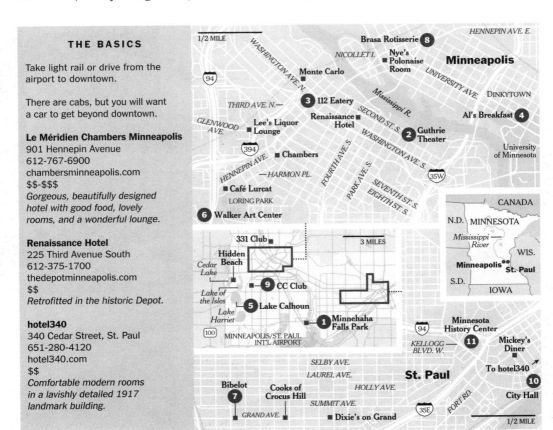

THE BASICS

Take light rail or drive from the airport to downtown.

There are cabs, but you will want a car to get beyond downtown.

Le Méridien Chambers Minneapolis
901 Hennepin Avenue
612-767-6900
chambersminneapolis.com
$$-$$$
Gorgeous, beautifully designed hotel with good food, lovely rooms, and a wonderful lounge.

Renaissance Hotel
225 Third Avenue South
612-375-1700
thedepotminneapolis.com
$$
Retrofitted in the historic Depot.

hotel340
340 Cedar Street, St. Paul
651-280-4120
hotel340.com
$$
Comfortable modern rooms in a lavishly detailed 1917 landmark building.

Duluth

Believe it. Minnesota bakes in the summer. And when temperatures hit the 90s, many Minnesotans head for Duluth, a port city on the westernmost tip of Lake Superior that is cooled to comfort by lakeshore breezes. Built into bluffs overlooking this largest of the Great Lakes, Duluth has long been the port gateway to Minnesota's Iron Range. Today, the spacious Victorian mansions built by mining and lumber barons are bed-and-breakfasts or museums. (The city may be better known as the childhood of Bob Dylan.) And the development of Canal Park, once an abandoned warehouse district, has given Duluth a vibrant waterfront of shops, bars, and restaurants.
— BY PAT BORZI

FRIDAY

1 *Lakefront Ramble* 5 p.m.

Acquaint yourself with **Canal Park** and the harbor by strolling the **Lakewalk**, a three-mile path along the Lake Superior shore. Whether you go the whole way or only part of it, rest your feet and enjoy the view from the deck of the **Sunset Grill** in the **Fitger's Brewery Complex** (600 East Superior Street; 218-722-8826; fitgers.com), a mile from Canal Park. A big brewery from 1859 until 1972, Fitger's was converted into shops, restaurants, and a luxury hotel and now houses a microbrewery. It's a great place to have a drink and watch the hulking ore boats inch in and out of the harbor. Too tired to walk back? Hop the Port Town Trolley, which serves Canal Park and the downtown hotels until about 7 p.m. in summer.

2 *What, No Ping?* 7 p.m.

They use real wooden bats in the Northwoods League, whose 12 teams of collegians serve as the Upper Midwest's answer to the Cape Cod Baseball League. The Duluth Huskies play at cozy **Wade Municipal Stadium** (101 North 35th Avenue West; 218-786-9909), a Works Projects Administration relic that opened in 1941. Tickets are cheap, and families have a great time.

OPPOSITE The former Fitger's Brewery Complex now holds shops, restaurants, a hotel, and a microbrewery.

RIGHT The Lake Superior Railroad Museum.

3 *The Lake Superior Sound* 10:30 p.m.

Some longtime Duluth residents say the local music scene isn't what it used to be. That may be, but Duluth offers plenty of late-night options. For one of the best combinations of music and food, hit **Pizza Lucé** (11 East Superior Street; 218-727-7400; pizzaluce.com; $$), where local and out-of-town bands play often and which serves delectable pizzas, pasta, and hot hoagies until 2:30 a.m. on weekends.

SATURDAY

4 *Breakfast at Mom's* 10 a.m.

Few places in Duluth do breakfast as well as the **Amazing Grace Bakery Café** (394 South Lake Avenue; 218-723-0075; amazinggraceduluth.com; $), in the basement of the **DeWitt-Seitz Marketplace** in Canal Park. The funky interior is a hoot. If your mother ever had plastic tablecloths with designs of oranges, apples, and peaches on them, she'd love this place. Try French toast, muffins, or scones.

5 *Mansion with a Past* 11:30 a.m.

Of all the captains of industry who once called Duluth home, Chester A. Congdon was one of the richest. **Glensheen** (3300 London Road; 218-726-8910; glensheen.org), his baronial 39-room lakefront mansion on almost eight acres, was completed in 1908. The basic tour of the main house's lower floors takes about an hour. An expanded tour includes the Arts and Crafts collection on the third floor. At one time tour guides were discouraged from discussing

to 1978, the *Irvin* (350 Harbor Drive; 218-722-5573; decc.org) is named for the former U.S. Steel president who occasionally sailed on it himself. The tour takes you through the engine room, the immense hold that could handle up to 14,000 tons of iron ore and coal, and the officers' and crew's quarters. Note the contrast of the stark crew's rooms with the stunning walnut-paneled staterooms for big-shot passengers.

8 *Tequila Sunset* 6 p.m.

Scoring a table at its elevated deck is the tough part at **Little Angie's Cantina** (11 East Buchanan Street; 218-727-6117; grandmasrestaurants.com/littleangies; $$), Canal Park's best spot for people-watching. Once you've done that, you can choose from Angie's 60-plus brands of tequila. Its margaritas come in three sizes. The largest, the 45-ounce mucho, goes well with almost anything on the menu.

9 *Ironman Gelato* 8 p.m.

Sometimes the iron ore didn't make it out of Duluth, and one relic of those days is **Clyde Iron Works** (2920 West Michigan Street; 218-727-1150; clydeparkduluth.com), once a foundry complex that turned out heavy equipment for logging and construction. Today it's a cavernous space that

the double murder committed at the estate in 1977. An intruder smothered the 83-year-old heiress to the Congdon family fortune with a pink satin pillow and beat her night nurse to death with a candlestick holder. Most guides now mention the crime, but you may not hear about it unless you ask.

6 *A View from the Wall* 2 p.m.

Grandma's Saloon & Grill (522 Lake Avenue South; 218-727-4192; grandmasrestaurants.com/retail.htm) is a popular Canal Park destination. Its deck overlooks the century-old Aerial Lift Bridge, where the roadway rises in one piece to let ore and grain boats pass. But it's more fun to grab a single-scoop waffle cone at **Grandma's Ice Cream Boxcar**, the grill's ice cream and soda stand across the parking lot, and join the crowd along the canal wall and watch these huge vessels go by. Wave to the deckhands — they'll wave back — but don't be the one who jumps when the ship sounds its horn.

7 *The Iron Boats* 3:30 p.m.

The doomed ore freighter *Edmund Fitzgerald*, sunk in a storm on Lake Superior in 1975 and immortalized in song by Gordon Lightfoot, departed from Superior, Wisconsin, across the harbor from Duluth. To get a sense of proportion, tour the immense **William A. Irvin**, a 610-foot retired laker that is still 110 feet shorter than the Fitzgerald. The flagship of U.S. Steel's Great Lakes Fleet from 1938

ABOVE AND BELOW Glensheen, a baronial mansion on the Lake Superior waterfront, belonged to Chester A. Congdon, one of Duluth's captains of industry. If your tour guide doesn't bring it up, ask about the double murder committed at the estate in 1977.

holds a restaurant, bakery, and events hall. Catch some live music or at least dig into a homemade baked dessert or gelato.

SUNDAY

10 *Railway History* 10 a.m.

Hop the trolley to the Depot, also known as the **Lake Superior Railroad Museum** (506 West Michigan Street; 218-727-8025; lsrm.org), and relive Duluth's rich railroad history. Beneath the former Union Depot, which in its heyday handled seven railroads and up to 50 trains a day, lies one of the country's most extensive collections of old locomotives, coaches, and other equipment. The admission price also gets you into the

rest of the St. Louis County Heritage and Arts Center, which includes a children's museum and a gallery.

11 *Just an Embryo* Noon

The **Electric Fetus** (12 East Superior Street; 218-722-9970; electricfetus.com) is a record shop as eccentric as its name suggests. If you absolutely have to get your toddler a Dead Kennedys T-shirt, this is the place to find it. The original Fetus opened in Minneapolis in 1968, and in many ways this branch remains stuck in time: for starters, the store smells like incense. The Fetus is known for offering CD's across every genre, and even if you don't buy anything on your way out of town, you should get a laugh out of looking at the buttons and headshop merchandise.

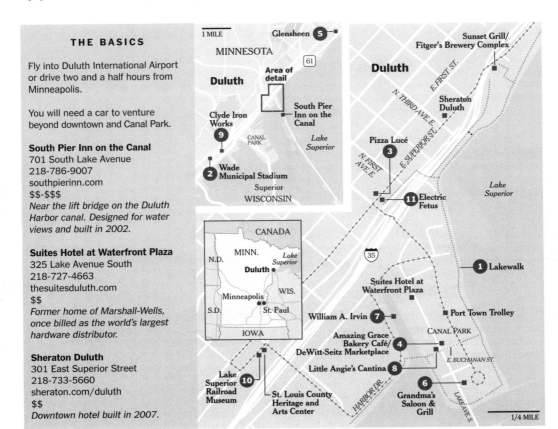

THE BASICS

Fly into Duluth International Airport or drive two and a half hours from Minneapolis.

You will need a car to venture beyond downtown and Canal Park.

South Pier Inn on the Canal
701 South Lake Avenue
218-786-9007
southpierinn.com
$$-$$$
Near the lift bridge on the Duluth Harbor canal. Designed for water views and built in 2002.

Suites Hotel at Waterfront Plaza
325 Lake Avenue South
218-727-4663
thesuitesduluth.com
$$
Former home of Marshall-Wells, once billed as the world's largest hardware distributor.

Sheraton Duluth
301 East Superior Street
218-733-5660
sheraton.com/duluth
$$
Downtown hotel built in 2007.

Traverse City

Driving along the fingerlike peninsulas of Grand Traverse Bay, it's easy to see why this part of Michigan calls itself the cherry capital. In spring, dense orchards explode in creamy blossoms, their pink hues like Impressionist smudges against the brilliant blue of Lake Michigan; come July's harvest time, the branches are thick with ruby fruit. But sprouting from the rolling green hillsides between the orchards is evidence of yet another fruitful enterprise — neat rows of vineyards that are drawing oenophiles and casual wine tasters alike. Around Grand Traverse Bay and in its urban center, Traverse City, are ample opportunities to experience both, with plenty of shopping, dining, and historic stop-offs — not to mention more than a hundred miles of sparkling waterfront — along the way.
— BY BETH GREENFIELD

FRIDAY

1 *Cherry Picking* 4 p.m.

Cherries are a prominent theme on Front Street in Traverse City, a pleasantly hip town that is also home to the weeklong summer National Cherry Festival. Amid the galleries, antiques, stores, and shops is the **Cherry Stop** boutique (211 East Front Street; 231-929-3990; cherrystop.com), stocked with cherry pie, cherry-pepper jam, cherry-scented candles, cherry-chipotle sauce, cherry body lotion, cherry cookbooks, and aprons bearing bold cherry prints. For cherry ice cream, choose **Kilwin's** (231-946-2403; 129 East Front Street; kilwins.com), which also proffers fat slabs of fudge.

2 *Creative Reuse* 6 p.m.

Another constellation of shops worth exploring resides in an unlikely place: within the Victorian Italianate brick walls of the former Northern Michigan Asylum for the Insane, founded in 1885 and redeveloped over the past few years into the retail and residential **Village at Grand Traverse Commons**. A slightly eerie vibe remains on the sprawling grounds, but inside the buildings you'll find a labyrinth of cool and quirky spots like **Creation**

OPPOSITE Sailing Grand Traverse Bay during the Michigan Schooner Festival.

Pharm (800 Cottageview Drive, Suite 45; 231-929-1100; creationpharm.com), with homemade soaps; **Gallery Fifty** (800 Cottageview Drive, Suite 50; 231-932-0775; galleryfifty.com), showing mixed-media works by local artists; and **Left Foot Charley** (806 Red Drive, Suite 100; 231-995-0500; leftfootcharley.com), an urban winery offering tastes of its Rieslings, pinot blancs, pinot grigios, and Gewurztraminers.

3 *Notes from the Underground* 7:30 p.m.

Settle in for dinner at **Trattoria Stella** (830 Cottageview Drive, Suite G-01; 231-929-8989; stellatc.com; $$–$$$), located in the surprisingly romantic former asylum cellar. Its contemporary Italian menu has a local focus, offering dishes like baked lasagna with roasted squash and shiitake mushrooms — not to mention an extensive wine list.

SATURDAY

4 *Protein Fix* 9 a.m.

Slide into a booth at the **Omelette Shoppe** (1209 East Front Street; 231-946-0590; omeletteshoppe.com; $), where options for the signature breakfast range from simple (western, Greek) to over-the-top (Chicken Fajita, with chicken, pepper, onions, avocado, cheese, and sour cream).

5 *Sip Sliding Away* 11 a.m.

Head due north out of the city onto the **Old Mission Peninsula**, a 22-mile strip that's narrow enough in stretches to let you drive up its spine while taking in bay views in both directions. Its length is a stretch of gently rolling hills, maple syrup stands, red barns, B&Bs, and cherry orchards — as well as several wineries, including the **Chateau Grand Traverse** (12239 Center Road; 231-223-7355; cgtwines.com) and **Chateau Chantal** (15900 Rue de Vin; 800-969-4009; chateauchantal.com), both of which have guest houses with rooms overlooking the vineyards. All offer daily tastings of their Rieslings and pinot noirs and, naturally, some version or other of a cloying cherry port.

6 *Lunch with a View* 1 p.m.

The **Old Mission General Store** (18250 Mission Road; 231-223-4310; oldmissiongeneralstore.com), should not be missed. It opened in a wigwam in

1839 as the first trading post between Detroit and Mackinac Island. Jim Richards, a former actor, now runs the place, his days onstage and in soap operas still evident in his booming voice and jaunty derby (it's a store rule that all the male workers wear period hats). There are creaky wood floors, big barrels of peanuts, an antique Victrola, and a heavy, ancient telephone whose receiver Richards picks up when it ding-a-lings — plus modern additions like store-made cherry salsa, steaming cups of chai, and fat Italian sandwiches. Order a couple and take them to the peninsula's northern tip for a picnic at a latitude of almost exactly 45 degrees north, halfway between the Equator and the North Pole. Stroll onto wide, muddy flats and peer out to the bay or back inland, where a clutch of furry pine trees hugs a tiny white church, a squat 1870 lighthouse, and the **Hesler Log House**, an 1856 residence constructed from hand-hewn pines and hemlocks and restored for visitors, complete with a faux cherry pie on a windowsill.

7 *Sweet and Dry* 2 p.m.

Loop back down Old Mission and then up the longer and wider **Leelanau Peninsula**, exploring winding country roads and precious little towns like **Suttons Bay**, with a neat row of restaurants and boutiques, and blink-and-you'll-miss-it **Lake Leelanau**. And certainly keep up the vino theme; Leelanau's 18 wineries include both the large **Black Star Farms** (10844 East Revold Road, Suttons Bay; 231-944-1270; blackstarfarms.com), where visitors sample pinot noir, brandy, and cheeses in a sun-drenched tasting room, and many smaller

ABOVE Farming with a view on the Leelenau Peninsula.

RIGHT You'll find an artists' community in Leland, where the prime attraction is Fishtown, a Lilliputian commercial-fishing post. Worn wooden docks and ramshackle structures hold shops and studios.

OPPOSITE Cherries on the tree near Traverse City.

vintners. "Go off a side road and through the woods and you'll find a vineyard here, a vineyard there, hundreds of acres of new vineyards," said Joel Goldberg, editor of the Detroit-based online consumer guide MichWine.com, who spoke between sips at the small **Chateau Fontaine** (2290 South French Road, Lake Leelanau; 231-256-0000; chateaufontaine.com).

8 *Fish Tales* 4 p.m.

You'll find an artists' community in **Leland**, where the prime attraction is **Fishtown**, a Lilliputian commercial-fishing post. Its worn wooden docks and ramshackle structures hold tiny clothing shops, a sunny pottery studio, and seafood stores like **Carlson's**, which sells fresh and smoked fish (205 West River; 231-256-9801). Fishing boats, both working and tourist, come and go, as do the Manitou Islands ferries, carrying gear-laden campers and hikers.

9 *Gone the Sun* 6 p.m.

This peninsula's tip, **Northport**, has a lighthouse, too — the red-roofed and climbable **Grand Traverse Lighthouse**, whose interior has been restored to its 1920s style. It's in the 1,300-acre **Leelanau State Park** (leelanaustatepark.com), with hiking paths and a leafy campground. The park fronts Lake Michigan, stretching out west toward Wisconsin, where you'll glimpse the perfect sunset to wind up your day.

10 *From Lake and Garden* 8 p.m.

From there, head back to the Old Mission Peninsula and the bayfront **Boathouse Restaurant**

(14039 Peninsula Drive, Traverse City; 231-223-4030; boathouseonwestbay.com; $$–$$$), where the chef prepares French-infused local-seasonal meals including creative takes on pan-seared lake perch. The choice of wines will make your head spin before you've had a sip.

SUNDAY

11 *Farewell Song* 11 a.m.

Ten minutes northeast of Traverse City, the quirky **Music House Museum** (7377 Route 31 North, Acme; 231-938-9300; musichouse.org) in a converted 1908 barn houses a collection of automatic musical instruments including a 1924 Wurlitzer theater organ,

a gorgeous 1917 Estey pipe organ, and an 18-foot-high Mortier dance organ from Belgium, hand-carved out of rosewood in 1922 and sounding like a full, festive band. A walnut and gold-leaf reproducing piano plays rolls remade from those created by George Gershwin. "This is exactly how he played *Rhapsody in Blue,*" explained a museum guide, Jack Pechur. And for nearly five minutes the keyboard dipped and heaved, ghostlike, through the piece, filling the soaring space with romantic sounds.

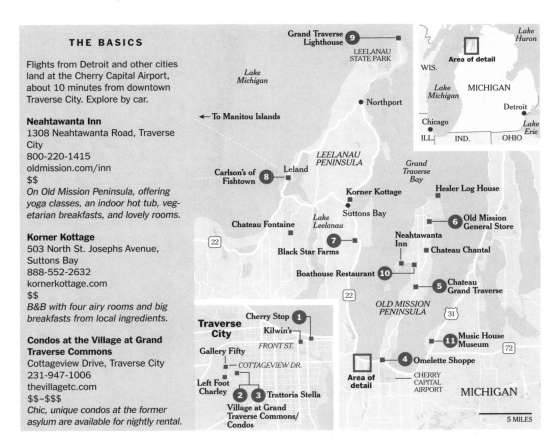

THE BASICS

Flights from Detroit and other cities land at the Cherry Capital Airport, about 10 minutes from downtown Traverse City. Explore by car.

Neahtawanta Inn
1308 Neahtawanta Road, Traverse City
800-220-1415
oldmission.com/inn
$$
On Old Mission Peninsula, offering yoga classes, an indoor hot tub, vegetarian breakfasts, and lovely rooms.

Korner Kottage
503 North St. Josephs Avenue, Suttons Bay
888-552-2632
kornerkottage.com
$$
B&B with four airy rooms and big breakfasts from local ingredients.

Condos at the Village at Grand Traverse Commons
Cottageview Drive, Traverse City
231-947-1006
thevillagetc.com
$$–$$$
Chic, unique condos at the former asylum are available for nightly rental.

Ann Arbor

It is not just the football season throngs of University of Michigan students dressed in maize and blue singing "Hail to the Victors" that make Ann Arbor the ultimate college town. Nor is it Michigan Stadium, with the largest attendance in the country (114,000 at some games), and renovated to the tune of $226 million. Rather it is the urban sophistication of this town — with its mix of restaurants, bars, boutiques, art-house movie theaters, and world-class art museums — that keeps many University of Michigan alumni from leaving long after they have graduated. For travelers, the sheer energy and the abundance of cultural opportunities, from classical dance performances to bluegrass concerts, makes a visit here a good time to get into the college spirit, even if it's not football season.
— BY JENNIFER CONLIN

FRIDAY

1 *Old-Time Shopping* 2 p.m.

Start your weekend in **Nickels Arcade**, an elegant glass-covered atrium that opened in 1918 and still houses businesses dating back 90 years. **Van Boven Clothing** (326 South State Street; 734-665-7228; vanboven.com) is a men's clothier that has long catered to well-dressed fraternity boys. The intimate **Comet Coffee** (16 Nickels Arcade; 734-222-0579) brews with beans grown from Ethiopia to El Salvador, one cup at a time. Then cross State Street to **Moe's Sport Shop** (711 North University Avenue; 734- 668-6915; moesportshops.com) to suit up as a Michigan fan. "U of M" apparel has been sold here since 1915, and you'll find such items as T-shirts and temporary "M" face tattoos.

2 *Student Scene* 3 p.m.

The **Diag**, as the open space on the central campus is called, is a leafy oasis intersected by sidewalks connecting academic buildings. Relax on a bench and take in the student scene, featuring everything from charity bucket drives to Ultimate Frisbee games. Just don't step on the brass inlaid "M" in front of the Harlan Hatcher Graduate Library—lore has it that freshmen who step on it will earn an F on their first exam. Then visit the architecturally stunning **Michigan Law School quadrangle** (625 South State Street), which could easily stand in for Harry Potter's Hogwarts, as could the library's Reading Room, with its vaulted ceilings, oak wainscoting, and stained glass windows.

3 *New Nostalgia* 5 p.m.

Between the Law School and the Ross School of Business you'll find **Dominick's** (812 Monroe Street; 734-662-5414), which has been serving students and the area's aging hippie population ever since the '60s, when the town was at the forefront of the Vietnam War protest movement. Though its picnic tables and booths are increasingly filled with entrepreneurs and M.B.A. candidates, everyone seems to enjoy the sangria served in jam jars on the patio. But avoid the temptation to eat here; instead head to **Mark's Carts** (markscartsannarbor.com) — a jumble of inexpensive ethnic food carts in a cozy courtyard on Washington Street between First and Ashley Streets, where, on Friday evenings, you can eat paella or tangy Thai slaw while listening to jazz, folk, and rock performers.

4 *Cool Culture* 8 p.m.

The University Musical Society (ums.org) offers a range of dance, theater, and musical productions performed at places that include the Hill Auditorium, with its superb acoustics, and the small but elegant Lydia Mendelssohn Theater. But it is the **Ark** (316 South Main Street; 734-761-1818; theark.org), one of North America's oldest nonprofit acoustic music clubs, that

OPPOSITE In football season, Michigan Stadium reverberates with cheering, roaring, and the school fight song.

RIGHT The Lunch Room, a vegan option at Mark's Carts, where you can catch live music on Friday evenings.

has developed an international reputation, not just for preserving American music (folk and bluegrass, in particular), but also for showcasing world music from Africa, the Caribbean, and elsewhere.

SATURDAY

5 *Sunny Side Up* 9 a.m.

Beat the crowds at **Angelo's** (1100 Catherine; 734-761-8996; angelosa2.com; $), where thick slices of raisin toast are second only to the pumpkin pancakes. Work off the calories with a brisk walk to the **Farmers' Market** (315 Detroit Street; 734-794-6255). Browse your way through stalls stocked with local products from fruit-flavored syrups (rhubarb, peach, cantaloupe) to wooden bird houses.

6 *Patience and Pumpernickel* Noon

Don't be put off by the line outside **Zingerman's** deli (422 Detroit Street; 734-663-3354; zingermansdeli.com; $$). Waiting is part of the experience. The friendly servers hand out nibbles of fresh bread, cheese, and brownies while you decide which of the 99 sandwiches you want (most popular: Zingerman's Reuben on Jewish rye). Or cross the street to **Monahan's Seafood Market** (407 North Fifth Avenue; 734-662-5118; monahansseafood.com; $) for an oyster po' boy or fresh chowder.

7 *Fun in the Big House* 1 p.m.

Kickoff time varies between noon and 4 p.m., depending on the college football broadcast schedule. Don't show up at the **Big House**, as the stadium is called, ticketless. Buying seats in advance (mgoblue.com) is a must. Though alcohol is not allowed, there is plenty of spirit in the cheering

ABOVE Saturday breakfast at Angelo's involves coffee, eggs, and thick slices of raisin toast.

OPPOSITE It's not all football at the University of Michigan. Serious reading takes place in this law school library.

of "Let's Go Blue" and the tunes played by the Michigan Marching Band. If you're here on one of the 45 or so weekends each year when there's no football game, don't despair. Find out how well Ann Arbor fits its name by checking out the trees, both native and exotic, in an afternoon ramble around **Nichols Arboretum** (1610 Washington Heights; 734-647-8986; lsa.umich.edu/mbg). It's a 123-acre site with panoramic views and a path along the winding Huron River.

8 *Cocktail Crawl* 5 p.m.

Whether Michigan has won or lost, students hit the bars. Avoid South University and State Street (student hubs) and head to the more civilized **Ann Street** (the place Bob Seger, who grew up in Ann Arbor, is actually singing about in the song "Mainstreet"). With dozens of night spots, it's easy to find a martini or microbrew; one favorite is **Palio** (347 South Main; 734-456-3463; paliorestaurant.com), where postgame parties erupt on the rooftop bar.

9 *The Global Gourmet* 7 p.m.

If it's ethnic food you crave, try **Pacific Rim** (114 West Liberty Street; 734-662-9303; pacificrimbykana.com; $$$) whose pan-Asian menu may include a delicate tuna tartare or pan-seared quinoa-crusted scallops. Head to **Logan** (115 West Washington Street; 734-327-2312; logan-restaurant.com; $$$) for dishes like Gruyère custard with caramelized onions and tomatoes or wild boar Bolognese. If you want a quick bite, **Frita Batidos** (117 West Washington Street; 734-761-2882; fritabatidos.com; $) serves Cuban specialties like fritas, spicy burgers of chorizo, black bean, white fish, beef, or turkey on a soft brioche. Batidos, fresh fruit shakes, are made with sweetened milk and crushed ice—with rum an optional addition.

10 *Wild at Dark* 9 p.m.

Housed in an old brewery, the **Cavern Club** (210 South First Street; 734-913-8890; cavernclubannarbor.com) attracts some of the biggest bands and D.J.'s from metro Detroit. Or you may prefer an evening at the **Michigan Theater** (603 East Liberty Street; 734-668-8463; michtheater.org). Opened in 1928 as a vaudeville and silent movie palace, it now offers live entertainment (the Ann

Arbor Symphony performs here regularly), as well as independent films. Night owls will appreciate the Saturday midnight shows of cult classics like *The Rocky Horror Picture Show* at the nearby **State Theater**, an Art Deco cinema built in 1942 (233 South State Street; 734-761-8667; michtheater.org/state).

SUNDAY

11 *Feed Body and Soul* 10:30 a.m.

Café Zola (112 West Washington Street; 734-769-2020; cafezola.com; $$) offers an eclectic menu that borrows from French, Italian, and Turkish cuisines — the crepes are both savory and sweet, and Turkish eggs are made with feta, spinach,

tomato, olives, and cucumber. Next, experience another kind of eclecticism at the **University of Michigan Museum of Art** (525 South State Street; 734-764-0395; umma.umich.edu). With more than 18,000 works — European, African, Asian, American, and Middle Eastern — it has something for everyone. For a different museum experience, cross the street to the **Kelsey Museum of Archaeology** (No. 434; 734-764-9304; lsa.umich.edu/kelsey), which holds thousands of ancient finds from the Mediterranean and Middle East.

THE BASICS

Ann Arbor is 45 miles west of Detroit and 35 miles north of the Ohio state line. Fly to the Detroit airport and take a cab to Ann Arbor, where you can explore on foot.

The Bell Tower
300 South Thayer Street
734-769-3010
belltowerhotel.com
$$
A charming hotel located right on campus and close to downtown.

The Inn at the League
911 North University Avenue
734-764-3177
uunions.umich.edu/league/inn
$$
A true campus experience, with wonderful views of the grounds, several dining spots, and a garden.

Dahlmann Campus Inn
615 East Huron Street
734-769-2200
campusinn.com
$$$
Conveniently located close to the university and downtown.

Ann Arbor

1/4 MILE

Huron River

BEAKES ST.

DETROIT ST.

FULLER ST.

CANADA

MICH.

WIS.

Detroit

Ann Arbor

Monahan's Seafood Market

6 Zingerman's

Farmers' Market

N. FIFTH AVE.

N. DIVISION ST.

N. STATE ST.

Ann Street

8

CATHERINE ST.

Mark's Carts

Cavern Club

10

11 Café Zola

Dahlmann Campus Inn

E. HURON ST.

5

Angelo's

State Theater

The Bell Tower

Frita Batidos/ Logan

E. WASHINGTON ST.

University Musical Society/Hill Auditorium

9 Pacific Rim

Michigan Theater

4

W. LIBERTY ST.

Ark

E. LIBERTY ST.

Moe's Sport Shop

S. FIRST ST.

S. MAIN ST.

Palio

Nickels Arcade/ Van Boven Clothing / Comet Coffee

1

The Inn at the League

2

N. UNIVERSITY AVE.

Diag

Kelsey Museum of Archaeology

1/2 MILE

Huron River

Area of detail

Nichols Arboretum

University of Michigan Museum of Art

Michigan Law School

Ann Arbor

S. STATE ST.

S. MONROE ST.

3 Dominick's

PACKARD ST.

S. MAIN ST.

Big House

7

PACKARD ST.

E. STADIUM BLVD.

HILL ST.

Detroit

Eminem celebrated Detroit, Michigan, in a slick Super Bowl commercial. Glenn Beck denigrated it by comparing it to Hiroshima. To visit Detroit these days is to experience both ends of that spectrum — a once great metropolis worn down by decades of corruption and economic woes, and a city fueled by newfound hope and enthusiasm as it painstakingly rebuilds itself. Edgy cafes and shops cater to young artists and professionals moving into downtown loft spaces. Established restaurants, museums, and musical venues recapture the storied past. You may have to work a little to find the best of Detroit, but it's worth it.
— BY JENNIFER CONLIN

FRIDAY

1 *Groove Time* 2 p.m.

Get into the beat of Detroit immediately with a visit to the **Motown Historical Museum** (2648 West Grand Boulevard; 313-875-2264; motownmuseum.com), where the tour guides are nearly as entertaining as the artists who first recorded their songs here at Berry Gordy Jr.'s recording studio, Hitsville USA, in the early 1960s. The memorabilia ranges from Marvelettes album covers to the Jackson Five's psychedelic bell bottoms. You can't help but sing the tunes of Marvin Gaye, Stevie Wonder, Diana Ross, Smokey Robinson, the Four Tops, and the Temptations as you wander into Studio A, where it all began.

2 *French Flavor* 5 p.m.

Though it is easy to forget this city's French colonial roots, at **Good Girls Go to Paris Crepes** (15 East Kirby Street, Suite 115; 877-727-4727; goodgirlsgotopariscrepes.com; $), Le Détroit feels alive and well in a setting of dark red walls and classic French movie posters. Try a Celeste (Brie, dried cranberries, and roast beef) or a Claire (chicken, broccoli, and Cotswold cheese), and leave room for an ooh-la-la dessert crepe. After dinner, stroll over to the elegant **Detroit Institute of Arts** (5200 Woodward Avenue; 313-833-7900; dia.org), which stays open until 10 p.m. on Fridays. There are works by Picasso and van Gogh, but the don't-miss is Diego Rivera's *Detroit Industry* fresco cycle from the 1930s.

3 *Cool Cat Cafe* 10 p.m.

Don't let the abandoned buildings or strip joint across the street keep you from **Café D'Mongo's** (1439 Griswold Street; cafedmongos.com), a wonderfully eccentric speakeasy that feels more like a private party than a bustling bar. The owner, Larry Mongo, is like a funky Mr. Rogers who knows everyone in the neighborhood and beyond, from the young "creative class" that frequents his establishment to the glamorous sixty-something women sipping dark cocktails at the bar. Live jazz and country music play on alternating Friday nights. Café D'Mongo's is open only on Fridays and occasionally, if the owner feels like it, the last Saturday of each month.

SATURDAY

4 *To Market* 8 a.m.

The six-block **Eastern Market** (2934 Russell Street; 313-833-9300; detroiteasternmarket.com), founded in 1891, is home to Detroit foodies with more than 250 vendors selling everything from fruits and vegetables to Michigan maple syrup and artisanal breads. This is also a great area for antiques and bric-a-brac. Try **Marketplace Antiques Gallery** (2047 Gratiot Avenue; 313-567-8250) or **Eastern Market Antiques** (2530 Market Street; 313-259-0600;

OPPOSITE The GM Renaissance Center downtown.

LEFT Hitsville USA, now the Motown Historical Museum. Wander into Studio A, where it all began for the likes of Marvin Gaye, Stevie Wonder, and Diana Ross.

easternmarketantiques.com). And if you have not sufficiently grazed your way through the market, stop in at the **Russell St. Deli** (2465 Russell Street; 313-567-2900; russellstreetdeli.com; $) for breakfast. The delicious raisin bread French toast is even better slathered with toasted pecans or fresh fruit.

5 *T Man* 10 a.m.

While Detroit has no shortage of historic homes and museums honoring the car industry, the **Model T Automotive Heritage Complex** (461 Piquette Avenue; 313-872-8759; tplex.org), the birthplace of the Model T Ford, stands out. This was Henry Ford's first factory, and it appears much as it did when it opened in 1904.

See various fully restored Model T's and visit the "secret experimental room" where Ford invented the car that would take motoring to the masses.

6 *Fire Up Your Belly* Noon

Located in Corktown, across the street from one of the saddest yet most historic landmarks in Detroit — the now abandoned Michigan Central Station — **Slows Bar B Q** (2138 Michigan Avenue; 313-962-9828; slowsbarbq.com; $$) is single-handedly revitalizing this area of the city with its baby back ribs, pulled pork, beef brisket, and chicken wings, as well as its charitable donations to local shelters, hospitals, and schools. Inside, the place is comfortable, with salvaged lumber, exposed brick walls, and a wrap-around bar. Outside, there may be a line, but Slows makes it worth taking a place at the end. What's more, waiting gives you a chance to dream up interesting development ideas for the haunting rail building in the distance.

7 *A Matinee Moment* 2 p.m.

The one thing not missing in this city is theaters — and they are housed in pristinely restored historic buildings. While away the afternoon with a performance in one of their classy interiors. On one weekend, matinee choices included a comedy at the intimate **Gem Theatre** (333 Madison Avenue; gemtheatre.com), a dance troupe at the

breathtakingly renovated **Detroit Opera House** (1526 Broadway; motopera.org), a Broadway musical at the **Fisher Theatre** (3011 West Grand Boulevard; broadwayindetroit.com), a children's show at the former movie palace the **Fox Theatre**, (2211 Woodward Avenue; olympiaentertainment.com), and a concert at **Music Hall** (350 Madison Avenue; musichall.org).

8 *Cheap and Cheerful* 6 p.m.

By far the best happy hour deal in town, and the crowds prove it, is at **Roast**, a modern brasserie located on the ground floor of the newly renovated Westin Book Cadillac Hotel (1128 Washington Boulevard; 313-961-2500; roastdetroit.com; $). Sidle up to the polished bar, settle onto a comfortable padded stool, and start ordering. You'll find beer, wine, and cocktails, and the bar food includes burgers, macaroni and cheese, and huge paper cones of hot fries.

9 *Jazz It Up* 9 p.m.

Cliff Bell's (2030 Park Avenue; 313-961-2543; cliffbells.com; $$) is one of the oldest and most famous supper clubs in Detroit (it originally opened in 1935), and after years of meticulous renovations, it is once again the place to be on a weekend night. Amid its Art Deco features, vaulted ceilings, mahogany bar, and mirrored walls, to say nothing of the sounds of the jazz ensembles performing each night, entering Cliff Bell's is like walking into a Fred Astaire film. With a

cocktail menu divided into two categories—Slippers (Dirty Detroit Martini, Gypsy Kiss) and Swizzlers (The Cliff Bell, Cumberland Cup)—food could easily be forgotten, but should not be. The menu ranges from filet mignon to shrimp and grits.

SUNDAY

10 *Art after Porridge* 10 a.m.

Atlas Global Bistro (3111 Woodward Avenue; 313-831-2241; atlasglobalbistro.com; $$) is located in the old Addison Hotel in the Brush Park district of Detroit and serves memorable brunch food—a duck and goat cheese omelet, for example, or wild rice porridge. When you're ready to move on, travel just up the street to the **Museum of Contemporary Art Detroit** (4454 Woodward Ave.; 313-832-6622; mocadetroit.org), housed in a former auto dealership. Exhibits explore emerging ideas in the contemporary art world, and the museum's store serves as a meeting

OPPOSITE ABOVE A survivor from 1911 at the Model T Automotive Heritage Complex, the birthplace of the Model T Ford. The building was Henry Ford's first factory and appears much as it did when it opened in 1904.

OPPOSITE BELOW Good Girls Go to Paris Crepes.

ABOVE The Detroit Opera House.

place for students at the neighboring College for Creative Studies.

11 *Potter's Paradise* 1 p.m.

Truly unique to Detroit is **Pewabic Pottery** (10125 East Jefferson Avenue; 313-626-2000; pewabic.org), a type of tile and vessel ware in unique glazes founded by ceramicist Mary Stratton during the Arts and Crafts movement in 1903. A National Historic Landmark, the building is now a production facility, museum,

and educational center with a store where eager fans, including Martha Stewart, still flock to buy ceramics. Take home a classic Pewabic tile, perhaps an acorn or a dragonfly.

ABOVE The Museum of Contemporary Art Detroit explores emerging art in a former auto dealership.

OPPOSITE The Italian Garden Room at the elegantly restored Book Cadillac Hotel, now a Westin.

THE BASICS

Detroit's airport receives flights from around the world. Walk and use taxis, which are cheap and plentiful.

Westin Book Cadillac Detroit
1114 Washington Boulevard
313-442-1600
bookcadillacwestin.com
$$
Landmark hotel built in 1924 and reopened in 2009 after a $200 million renovation.

Inn on Ferry Street
84 East Ferry Street
313-871-6000
innonferrystreetdetroit.com
$$
Four historic homes and two carriage houses connected as a charming inn.

Detroit Marriott at the Renaissance Center
400 Renaissance Drive
313-568-8000
marriott.com
$$
A 1,298-room skyscraper hotel at General Motors headquarters.

Toronto

As one of the planet's most diverse cities, Toronto is oddly clean and orderly. Sidewalks are spotless, trolleys run like clockwork, and the locals are polite almost to a fault. That's not to say that Torontonians are dull. Far from it. With a population that is now half foreign-born — fueled by growing numbers of East Indians, Chinese, and Sri Lankans — this city on the shore of Lake Ontario offers a kaleidoscope of world cultures. Sing karaoke in a Vietnamese bar, sip espresso in Little Italy, and catch a new Bollywood release, all in one night. The art and design scenes are thriving, too, and not just on the red carpets of the Toronto International Film Festival, held every September. Industrial zones have been reborn into gallery districts, and dark alleys now lead to designer studios, giving Canada's financial capital an almost disheveled mien. — BY DENNY LEE

FRIDAY

1 *West Enders* 4 p.m.

Toronto's cool scene seems to migrate west along Queen Street West every few years. It started out at Yonge Street, with punk rockers and art students pouring into sweaty clubs. Then, when mainstream stores like the Gap moved in, the scenesters fled west, past Bathurst Street, to a district now called **West Queen West** (westqueenwest.ca), where old appliance stores are still being carved into rough-hewn galleries and hunter-chic boutiques. Start your stroll along Toronto's art mile at Bathurst Street and go west. Raw spaces that showcase young Canadian artists include **Paul Petro Contemporary Art** (980 Queen Street West; 416-979-7874; paulpetro.com).

2 *Designer Meats* 8 p.m.

For a taste of hipsterdom, put on a T-shirt and squeeze into **OddFellows** (936 Queen Street West; 416-534-5244; oddfellows.ca; $$), a boutique-like bistro where the area's beard-and-flannel posse gathers nightly. The corner restaurant is run by Brian Richer and Kei Ng, partners in a maverick design firm,

OPPOSITE Santiago Calatrava's atrium at Brookfield Place has been described as the "crystal cathedral of commerce."

RIGHT Leslieville is packed with cafes and antiques shops.

Castor Design (castordesign.ca), known for elevating mundane materials into clever objects. The menu follows similar sleights of hand. Manly cuts are skillfully turned into Canadian comfort dishes like bison meatloaf and venison burgers. The long communal table, made of polished limestone and random legs, encourages chitchat.

3 *Trend North* 10:30 p.m.

Let the frat boys have College Street. And West Queen West has been overrun lately with 905ers, slang for out-of-towners with suburban area codes. The cool kids, it seems, are now migrating north along Ossington Avenue, which some Toronto bloggers are already calling Next West Queen West. Bookending the district are **Sweaty Betty's** (13 Ossington Avenue; 416-535-6861), a hole-in-the-wall with a brash jukebox, and **Communist's Daughter** (1149 Dundas Street West; 647-435-0103), an understated lounge. A trendy bar crawl is emerging in between, tucked among old Portuguese bakeries and kitchen supply stores.

SATURDAY

4 *Eggs and Egg Chairs* 10:30 a.m.

Brunch is serious business in this town, and discerning eaters are making their way to Leslieville, a once grimy neighborhood in East Toronto now packed with smart-looking cafes and midcentury-modern stores. Get your morning eggs at **Table 17** (782 Queen Street East; 416-519-1851; table17.ca; $$), a country-style French bistro. Afterward, look over well-priced and well-curated antiques shops like

Machine Age Modern (1000 Queen Street East; 416-461-3588; machineagemodern.com), which carries teak dining tables, Georg Jensen clocks, and other vintage modern treasures.

5 *O Calcutta* 2 p.m.

This is a city of minority neighborhoods, from the souvlaki joints in Greektown to the rainbow-hued windows of Gay Village. There are even two Chinatowns. But for color and spice, hop a taxi to Little India. The hilltop district spans just six blocks along Gerrard Street East, but it's jammed with more than a hundred stores and restaurants. Wander the shops and try the food. **Dubai Jewellers** (1407 Gerrard Street East; 416-465-1200) has a dazzling assortment of Indian-designed gold pieces. And for a midday snack, **Udupi Palace** (No. 1460; 416-405-8189; udupipalace.ca) is a bright restaurant that makes delicious dosas, chaats, and other South Indian treats.

6 *Made in Canada* 4 p.m.

Local fashion is disappointing, even in West Queen West. A handsome exception is **Klaxon Howl** (at the rear entrance of 694 Queen Street West; 647-436-6628; klaxonhowl.com), a homegrown men's label that blends vintage military gear with its own rugged work shirts, selvage denim jeans, and waxed cotton jackets. The design scene, on the other hand, is flourishing. For clever housewares, take a slight detour to **Made** (867 Dundas Street West; 416-607-6384; madedesign.ca), a gallery store that represents young product designers with a fresh and playful eye.

7 *Nomadic Tastes* 8 p.m.

A new culinary confidence has taken hold of Toronto. Not only are kitchens updating traditional Canadian fare like charcuterie and wild boar, but young chefs are tapping Toronto's global roots in ways that transcend standard fusion. Asian fusion restaurants like **Madeline's** (601 King Street West; 416-603-2205; susur.com/madelines) are busy. But also making a mark are hot spots like **Nyood** (1096

Queen Street West; 416-466-1888; nyood.ca; $), a pan-Mediterranean restaurant with big chandeliers and frilly molding. Dishes like the Malta braised short ribs are a hit, while tasty cocktails like the berry mojito keep the party going.

8 *Get Wiggy* 11 p.m.

O.K., College Street is not all bad, especially if you're single and in your mid-20s to 30s. A place to start is the unimaginatively named **College Street Bar** (No. 574; 416-533-2417; collegestreetbar.com). The dim space has brick walls, a woodsy patio, and a refreshing microbrew that draws a good-looking crowd of Web designers and writer types. Afterward, you can catch the 1 a.m. drag show at **El Convento Rico** (No. 750; 416-588-7800; elconventorico.com), a low-rent, high-octane club that attracts an exuberant mix of bachelorettes in plastic tiaras and muscular men with high voices.

SUNDAY

9 *Dim Sum Luxe* 11 a.m.

For inventive dim sum you won't find anywhere else, make a beeline for **Lai Wah Heen** (108 Chestnut Street; 416-977-9899; laiwahheen.com; $$$), a white-tablecloth restaurant on the second floor of the Metropolitan Hotel. Expect fanciful creations like

crab dumplings that resemble purple crabs and tofu paired with truffles and mushroom.

10 *Trophy Museum* 1 p.m.

The CN Tower notwithstanding, Toronto has impressive architecture by giants like Ludwig Mies van der Rohe, Santiago Calatrava, and Thom Mayne. But work by its favorite son, Frank Gehry, was missing until 2008, when the **Art Gallery of Ontario** (317 Dundas Street West; 416-979-6648; ago.net) reopened with a bold renovation by Gehry, who grew up just blocks from the century-old museum. He wrapped the original Beaux-Arts structure in sheets of billowing glass and swaths of Douglas fir, and added a spiraling wood staircase that pierces the glass roof to a new contemporary-art wing. It's a stunning homecoming for an architect credited with helping other cities flourish — not that Toronto needs a hand.

OPPOSITE ABOVE Street scene in Toronto.

OPPOSITE BELOW A staircase at Toronto's New City Hall, designed by Finnish architect Viljo Revell.

ABOVE Inside Klaxon Howl in the West Queen West district.

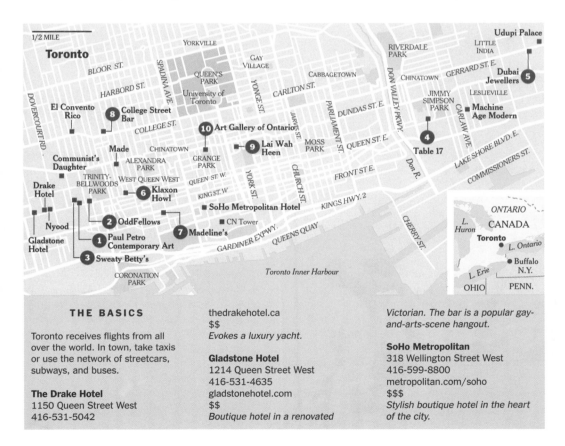

THE BASICS

Toronto receives flights from all over the world. In town, take taxis or use the network of streetcars, subways, and buses.

The Drake Hotel
1150 Queen Street West
416-531-5042

thedrakehotel.ca
$$
Evokes a luxury yacht.

Gladstone Hotel
1214 Queen Street West
416-531-4635
gladstonehotel.com
$$
Boutique hotel in a renovated

Victorian. The bar is a popular gay-and-arts-scene hangout.

SoHo Metropolitan
318 Wellington Street West
416-599-8800
metropolitan.com/soho
$$$
Stylish boutique hotel in the heart of the city.

Niagara Falls

At Niagara, the United States is the poor relation and Canada is king. Though they share the famous falls, Nature gave Canada the wide-angle view, and the Canadians' long-term bet on tourism over industry landed most of the visitor comforts on their side of the Niagara River. Yet the story isn't so simple. Casinos, high-rise hotels, and hucksterish come-ons have so proliferated in Niagara Falls, Ontario, that it risks feeling like a tired amusement park. Meanwhile, in Niagara Falls, New York, the visitor who ventures inside the shabby, underfunded state park is surprised to discover vestiges of something like a natural landscape. The party is in Canada. The real feel of the river, in all its awesome power, is more accessible in the United States. So why miss either one? It's an easy border to cross, especially on foot. Hop back and forth to get the best of both Niagaras and see for yourself.
— BY BARBARA IRELAND

FRIDAY

1 *Feet Across the Border* 5 p.m.

Cars sometimes line up for hours to cross the international border at the **Rainbow Bridge**, a few hundred yards downriver from the falls. But on the walkway it's a breeze—a 10-minute stroll for 50 cents in American or Canadian currency (niagarafallsbridges.com). Customs agents at each end are pedestrian-friendly, though you must have your passport. If you're staying on the American side, make your first crossing now. If your hotel is in Canada, wait until tomorrow. Either way, this is one of the most scenic saunters you will ever take.

2 *Brinkmanship* 6 p.m.

Push into the crowds on the riverfront walkway in Canada and see the whole geological spectacle at once. The imposing cascade on the left, 850 feet wide, is the **American Falls**. The supercharged one on the right, nearly half a mile wide, is the **Horseshoe Falls**, often called the Canadian Falls even though

OPPOSITE Niagara Falls State Park offers jaw-dropping up-close views of both the American and Canadian Falls.

RIGHT On the Canadian side of the Falls, Clifton Hill is a funhouse in and of itself.

the international border actually runs through it. Stop at the Horseshoe brink and wait your turn to be doused at the rail by spray from thousands of tons of water plunging down every second. Impressed? This thundering mass is only half of the river's natural flow. The other 50 percent (75 percent in the off-season) is channeled away underground to hydroelectric plants.

3 *Wine and Bacon* 7 p.m.

From the terrace at **Edgewaters Tap & Grill** (6345 Niagara Parkway; 905-356-2217; niagaraparks.com/dining; $$), the tourist hordes below seem far away. Relax and sample one of the Niagara Region wines, like the Inniskillin Riesling. For a casual dinner, try a hearty sandwich made with the high-quality Canadian bacon hard to find south of the border. Afterward, explore shady **Queen Victoria Park**, where gracious landscaping reflects the English style.

4 *Over the Top* 9 p.m.

You want to hate **Clifton Hill**, a garish strip of funhouses, glow-in-the-dark miniature-golf palaces, 4-D theaters, wax museums, and noisy bars. But tackiness on this level cries out to be experienced. So watch a multinational crowd shovel tickets into blinking game machines at the Great Canadian Midway. Observe the story-high monster chomping a hamburger atop the House of Frankenstein. Shop for maple candy and a moose puppet. And climb aboard the **SkyWheel** Ferris wheel (4950 Clifton Hill; cliftonhill.com) for five vertiginous revolutions and a view of the colored lights projected nightly on the falls. (Oh right, there are waterfalls here. Remember?)

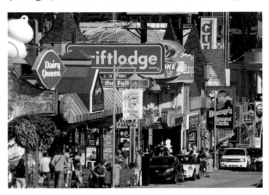

SATURDAY

5 *The Central Park* 10 a.m.

Frederick Law Olmsted and Frederic Church were among the 19th-century champions of a radical idea, public parks at Niagara Falls, erasing a clutter of factories and tourist traps (at some locations, visitors had paid to see the falls through a peephole in a fence). The Free Niagara movement succeeded on both sides of the border, and on the American side Olmsted designed landscapes at the crest of both waterfalls and on Goat Island, which separates them. Explore the woods and walkways of the resulting **Niagara Falls State Park** (716-278-1796; niagarafallsstatepark.com) to find what remains of the essential experience of Niagara. For an enticing mix of quiet glades and furious rapids, venture out on the tiny **Three Sisters Islands** above the thunderous Horseshoe.

6 *Wings Optional* 1 p.m.

Buffalo chicken wings were invented just 20 miles away, and the menu at the **Top of the Falls** restaurant (in the state park; 716-278-0337; $$) won't let you forget it. Partake or not; alternatives include salads, burgers, and wraps. Every table has a falls view.

7 *Why the Waterfall?* 2 p.m.

You'll hunt in vain on both sides of the river for a straightforward geological explanation of Niagara Falls. At the **Niagara Gorge Discovery Center** in the state park, look selectively at the displays and ask questions to tease out the basic facts. What's falling is the water of the Great Lakes. The falls are on the move upriver, naturally receding as much as 6 feet a year. There's a giant whirlpool where they took a sharp turn 40 centuries ago. (A Canadian attempt at explaining Niagara, a film called *Niagara's Fury*, niagarasfury.com, is entertaining for children but also not especially informative, mixing cartoon stereotypes with snippets of textbook language.) Outside the Discovery Center, a trail heads toward the deep Niagara Gorge, where hikers get within a few feet of the largest standing waves in North America. Don't bring the kayak: these rapids are Level 6.

8 *The Close-up* 3 p.m.

Many of the contrived attractions at Niagara Falls are overhyped and disappointing. But the **Maid of the Mist** tour boats (maidofthemist.com) have been thrilling customers since 1846. Chug out to the base of the Horseshoe on one of these sturdy craft, struggle to look up 170 feet to the top through the torrents, and you'll grasp the power of what brought you here. Go from the **American dock**. Not only is the wait likely to be shorter than on the Canadian side, but at the end of the ride, you can hang on to your flimsy slicker and take a wet but exhilarating hike to the base of the American Falls.

9 *Culinary Canada* 7 p.m.

AG, the soothing, stylish restaurant in the **Sterling Inn & Spa** (5195 Magdalen Street, Niagara Falls, Ontario; 289-292-0000; sterlingniagara.com; $$$) serves imaginative dishes using seasonal Canadian ingredients, paired with local wines. One

ABOVE The Rainbow Bridge, the international crossing, offers views of the American Falls — and Prospect Point Observation Tower, in the foreground.

BELOW Preparing to be soaked at the Cave of the Winds.

summer menu included basil-and-potato-encrusted Lake Huron trout and pork tenderloin stuffed with macerated Niagara fruit. The desserts are good, too, but if you're not up for one, you can get by on the eye candy of the red, white, and crystal dining room.

SUNDAY

10 *Vineyards Haven* 10 a.m.

Leave the falls behind and drive north along the river in Canada on the lovely **Niagara Parkway**. Beyond placid Queenston, where an American attack was turned back in the War of 1812, the Niagara turns tame, and wineries, peach orchards, manor-like houses, and an inviting bicycle path line the road. The tasting rooms pour chardonnays, pinot noirs, and the regional specialty, ice wine. At **Inniskillin**, (on the Parkway at Line 3; 905-468-9910; inniskillin.com) tours and signboards explain grape-friendly local conditions. **Reif Estate** (15608 Niagara Parkway; 905-468-9463; reifwinery.com) has a gimmicky but pleasant Wine Sensory Garden. **Peller Estates** (just off the parkway at 290 John Street West; peller.com) pairs its vintages with a posh restaurant. Between the reds and whites, stop in at the **Kurtz Orchards Gourmet Marketplace** (16006 Niagara Parkway; 905-468-2937; kurtzorchards.com), where you can munch enough free samples of breads, tapenades, jams, cheeses, and nut butters to take you all the way to dinner.

THE BASICS

By car, Niagara Falls is eight hours from New York City, 90 minutes from Toronto, and 45 minutes from the Buffalo Niagara airport. At the falls, walk and take trolleys and people movers. For exploring, drive a car.

Sterling Inn & Spa
5195 Magdalen Street, Niagara Falls, Ontario
877-783-7772
sterlingniagara.com
$$$
A boutique-hotel oasis at the edge of the tourist maelstrom.

Doubletree Fallsview Resort & Spa
6039 Fallsview Boulevard, Niagara Falls, Ontario
905-358-3817
niagarafallsdoubletree.com
$$
On a hill overlooking the falls.

The Giacomo
222 First Street, Niagara Falls, New York
716-299-0200
thegiacomo.com
$$$
Renovated Art Deco building.

CANADA
40 MILES
Lake Ontario
Toronto
Lake Ontario
ONTARIO
Rochester
Niagara Falls • Niagara Falls
Buffalo
390
Lake Erie
NEW YORK
90

Niagara-on-the-Lake
Peller Estates ■ Kurtz Orchards Gourmet Marketplace
Reif Estate — RIVER RD.
■
Inniskillin ■
10 Niagara Parkway

1/2 MILE
RIVER RD.
Niagara River
ROBERT — MOSES PKWY.
AG/ Sterling Inn & Spa Clifton Hill
9 4
7 Niagara Gorge Discovery Center
Doubletree Fallsview Resort & Spa SkyWheel
1 Rainbow Bridge
8 Maid of the Mist tour boats
Edgewaters Tap & Grill
3 ■
American Falls The Giacomo
5 Niagara Falls State Park
Top of the Falls 6
GOAT ISLAND
Queen Victoria Park Horseshoe Falls
2
Three Sisters Islands
UNITED STATES
CANADA

CANADA NEW YORK
Queenston
405
Whirlpool ■ 190
Niagara Falls
Niagara River
2 MILES

Buffalo

Prospering where East Coast railroads met Great Lakes cargo, Buffalo, New York, was a rich city around 1900, the same era when dynamic innovators were transforming American architecture. Wealth and vision came together in works by Frank Lloyd Wright, Louis Sullivan, H. H. Richardson, Frederick Law Olmsted, Eliel and Eero Saarinen, and more—arrayed amid blocks of Victorian houses and lavish mansions. When industry eventually collapsed, a shaken and considerably poorer Buffalo slowly realized it had a legacy. Now the city works to preserve its remarkable architectural collection and is eager to show it off. Visit in the months when Buffalo gets a glorious payback for its snowy winters with some of the best summer weather in the country. — BY BARBARA IRELAND

FRIDAY

1 *Lake to River* 2 p.m.

At **Erie Basin Marina** (329 Erie Street), a popular spot with sailors, joggers, and just about everyone else, climb the small observation tower for a view of grain elevators (a Buffalo invention) on the placid Buffalo River, an 1833 lighthouse, and the final expanse of Lake Erie as it narrows to become the Niagara River. The trees a couple of miles across the water are in Canada—British troops came across to burn Buffalo to the ground in the War of 1812, but all is now forgiven. To the north, the river current picks up on the way to Niagara Falls, 15 miles downstream. Climb back down and amble over to **Templeton Landing** (2 Templeton Terrace; 716-852-7337; templetonlanding.com; $$) for a drink and a sandwich on the waterfront patio.

2 *She's the Babe* 4 p.m.

Architectural preservation has achieved the status of a local religion, and the singer Ani DiFranco, a Buffalo native, made a creative contribution with **Babeville** (341 Delaware Avenue; 716-852-3835; babevillebuffalo.com), a towering 1876 red sandstone church adapted into a public event space and the headquarters of her Righteous Babe Records. To

get there, drive north on Delaware Avenue past the massive Art Deco City Hall and the McKinley Monument, a 96-foot-tall marble apology to the president who was assassinated while visiting Buffalo in 1901. Inside Babeville, look over the current show at **Hallwalls** (716-854-1694; hallwalls.org), a contemporary art gallery.

3 *The Temple of Wings* 8 p.m.

Take a table at the **Anchor Bar** (1047 Main Street; 716-886-8920; anchorbar.com; $), where the fame of Buffalo chicken wings began, for a plate of the spicy originals and the tale of their invention by a resourceful cook. Add a salad and some Canadian beer, and stay for live jazz.

SATURDAY

4 *Sullivan and Friends* 9:45 a.m.

See a microcosm of 19th-century American architecture in a downtown walking tour with Preservation Buffalo Niagara (617 Main Street; 716-852-3300; buffalotours.org). Louis Sullivan's 1895 **Guaranty Building** (28 Church Street), 13 stories of intricately molded terra cotta enclosing a steel skeleton, stands across a narrow street from **St. Paul's Cathedral** (128 Pearl Street), designed by Richard Upjohn, the architect of New York City's Trinity Church. Nearby, the Gothic Revival **Erie Community College** (121 Ellicott Street) was built in lavish style as a federal building when the city's friends included President Grover Cleveland, a former Buffalo mayor and briefly the town hangman. Daniel Burnham's elaborate **Ellicott Square Building** (295 Main Street) has been carefully preserved—from the Medusa heads peering out from its roof line perimeter to its refined interior atrium—by its current owner, Carl Paladino, who is better known for his boisterous 2010 campaign for governor of New York.

5 *Olmsted Next Door* Noon

Have a panini at the cafe in the **Albright-Knox Art Gallery** (1285 Elmwood Avenue; 716-882-8700; albrightknox.org) and then take a quick look around, concentrating on mid-20th-century paintings, where the collection is particularly strong. Seymour H.

OPPOSITE Daniel Burnham's Ellicott Square Building, one of Buffalo's many architectural gems.

Knox, a Buffalo banker and heir to part of the F. W. Woolworth fortune, was an early patron of Abstract Expressionists like Willem de Kooning, Mark Rothko, and, especially, Clyfford Still, and he gave the gallery hundreds of their works. Look out from the back portico, past the caryatids sculptured by Augustus Saint-Gaudens, at a view of 350-acre Delaware Park, the "central park" of an extensive system of parks and connecting parkways designed for Buffalo by Frederick Law Olmsted.

6 *Wright Writ Large* 2 p.m.

Frank Lloyd Wright liked nothing more than an open checkbook to work with, and when he designed a home in 1904 for Darwin Martin, a Buffalo business-man, in effect he had one. The result was the **Martin House Complex** (125 Jewett Parkway; 716-856-3858; darwinmartinhouse.org) — a sprawling 15,000-square-foot Prairie-style house filled with art glass and Wright-designed furniture, two smaller houses on the same property, a conservatory, stables, gardens, and a 100-foot-long pergola. A just-completed $50 million restoration has brought it back from long neglect and added an ethereally transparent visitor center designed by Toshiko Mori. Tour the complex, a stunningly beautiful and intricate work of art, and hear the stories. Martin absorbed outrageous cost overruns to give the master a free hand. He became a lifelong friend who bailed Wright out with tens of thousands of dollars in loans that were never repaid. (Their sizable correspondence is at the University at Buffalo.) Wright's obsession with detail extended to designing a dress for Mrs. Wright to wear in the house, but he resisted giving her a closet.

ABOVE A 19th-century grain elevator and a 21st-century marina in the Buffalo harbor.

LEFT The permanent collection at the Albright-Knox Art Gallery includes hundreds of Abstract Expressionist works.

7 *A Little Richardson* 4 p.m.

Back on Elmwood Avenue, drive south, past the **Burchfield-Penney Art Center** (burchfieldpenney.org), a gallery with a collection of eye-poppingly original paintings by the mystically inclined Charles Burchfield. Turn onto Forest Avenue and look behind a graceful screen of trees (another Olmsted landscape) for the majestic, spooky towers of the **H.H. Richardson Complex**. An abandoned mental hospital, it was one of Richardson's earliest and largest buildings in the style now known as Richardsonian Romanesque. Repairs have begun, but full restoration is a long way off.

8 *Retail Break* 4:30 p.m.

Shops are sprinkled along Elmwood Avenue from Bidwell Parkway to West Ferry Street. Browse through jewelry, clothing, and handcrafted curios at **Plum Pudding** (No. 779; 716-881-9748), or pick up a scarf or a Sarah Palin paper doll (her outfits include a moose-antler hat) at **Positively Main Street** (No. 773; 716-882-5858). **Talking Leaves** (No. 951; 716-884-9524; tleavesbooks.com) is a well-stocked independent bookstore. If you're not yet tired of National Historic

ABOVE A sailboat heads out toward open waters in Lake Erie from the Erie Basin Marina.

RIGHT Kleinhans Music Hall, designed by Eliel and Eero Saarinen, is home to the Buffalo Philharmonic.

Landmarks, drive a few blocks to the 1940 **Kleinhans Music Hall** (370 Pennsylvania Street), where Eliel and Eero Saarinen married upswept lines and near-perfect acoustics. Its carefully shaped wooden interior walls were "as warm as the wood in my violin," Isaac Stern once told an audience there.

9 *The French Style* 8 p.m.

Rue Franklin (341 Franklin Street; 716-852-4416; ruefranklin.com; $$$), whose reputation as Buffalo's best restaurant is rarely challenged, not only serves French wines and updated French food cooked by its French owner, but takes a French-style August vacation. If you're in town during its hiatus, try **Oliver's** (2095 Delaware Avenue; 716-877-9662; oliverscuisine.com; $$$), a favorite since 1936. At either one, expect a well-prepared meal and a relaxing evening.

SUNDAY

10 *Early to Betty's* 9 a.m.

The scones and coffee are great at **Betty's** (370 Virginia Street; 716-362-0633; bettysbuffalo.com; $), but there's more for breakfast, including spinach potato pancakes with bacon or scrambled tofu hash, served in a setting of brick walls and changing work by local artists. Get there early to beat the crowd.

11 *Wright on the Lake* 11:30 a.m.

It's a leisurely drive south along Lake Erie to **Graycliff** (6472 Old Lake Shore Road, Derby; 716-947-9217; graycliffestate.org), the summer house that Frank Lloyd Wright designed in the 1920s for Darwin Martin. The house and its lakeside setting are inspiring, but the story ends sadly here. Martin lost his fortune in the Great Depression, and his family eventually sold or abandoned all of their Wright-designed properties. Remarking on Martin's death in 1935, Wright said he had lost "my best friend."

OPPOSITE Gates Circle, a detail of Buffalo's parks and parkway system designed by Frederick Law Olmsted.

THE BASICS

Fly into Buffalo Niagara International Airport or drive 100 miles from Toronto or 400 miles from New York City.

A car is necessary.

The Mansion
414 Delaware Avenue
716-886-3300
mansionondelaware.com
$$$
Luxurious 28-room hotel in an elegant oversized house built in 1869.

Hyatt Regency Buffalo
300 Pearl Street
716-856-1234
buffalo.hyatt.com
$$
Built in and around a 1923 office building.

Embassy Suites Buffalo
200 Delaware Avenue
716-842-1000
embassysuitesbuffalo.com
$$$
Part of a gleaming 2005 multi-use development.

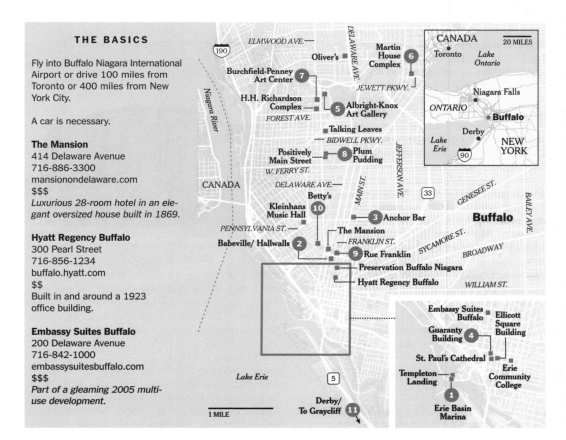

The Laurel Highlands

In the Laurel Highlands of southwestern Pennsylvania, cornfields undulate between forested slopes and rivers spill downward in a rush of whitewater, luring fishermen and rafters. These green hills gave Frank Lloyd Wright the setting for Fallingwater, his cantilevered masterpiece of a house set over a swiftly flowing creek. Nearby, another client hired Wright to design Kentuck Knob, a quirky counterpart. And a bit north in Acme, a Wright ranch house saved from demolition in Illinois arrived in pieces, completing the setting for a Wrightian weekend. Balancing the architectural immersion with a little history and some outdoor adventures creates a memorable experience under the shiny leaves of the mountain laurel.

— BY BETHANY SCHNEIDER AND BARBARA IRELAND

FRIDAY

1 *A Matter of Necessity* 4 p.m.

Everybody has to start somewhere, and George Washington's first battlefield command was in 1754 at what is now **Fort Necessity National Battlefield** (off Route 40 in Farmington; 724-329-5805; nps.gov/fone). The reconstruction of the fort that Washington's forces threw together in their moment of necessity (they were about to be attacked) is terrifying in its meagerness. Sure enough, the French and their Indian allies made mincemeat of the British led by Colonel Washington, then just 22. But other victories came later, and the French and Indian War made Washington's reputation. Rangers evoke the feel of combat in the era when these highlands were virgin forest, delivering dramatic lines like "Half King, Washington's Indian ally, washed his hands in the brains of the French commander."

2 *Dinner Downtown* 7 p.m.

Wash your own hands in something more appropriate as you tidy up for dinner. Find it in the old town center of Uniontown at **Caileigh's** (105 East Fayette Street; 724-437-9463; caileighs.com; $$).

OPPOSITE Frank Lloyd Wright's Fallingwater, the famed masterwork cantilevered over a waterfall in the woods of the Laurel Highlands.

RIGHT The Cucumber Falls at Ohiopyle State Park.

Uniontown was home to coal and steel barons in the boomtown days of this part of Pennsylvania, and Caileigh's occupies one of the era's mansions. As you settle in for dishes like spiced duck or seared grouper topped with Puerto Rican crab, chat with your waiter about General George C. Marshall, father of the Marshall Plan and Uniontown's favorite son.

SATURDAY

3 *The Masterwork* 8:15 a.m.

Arrive in plenty of time for your in-depth tour at **Fallingwater** (724-329-8501; fallingwater.org; tours must be purchased several weeks in advance). You're up early, but it's worth it; this tour, longer than the basic version, allows more time inside the house and more leisure to absorb the complexity of its construction. Projecting airily out over a waterfall on Bear Run Creek, its platforms mimicking the striations of the local rock, the house still looks as strikingly original and eerily perfect for its setting as it did when it was completed in 1939. Instantly famous, it resuscitated the faltering career of its creator, Frank Lloyd Wright, who was then 72. No matter how many times you've seen it, Fallingwater is breathtaking. On one bright May day, a middle-aged visitor from Scotland, dressed in a blue anorak, stood with tears flowing down his cheeks at his first sight of it. The guide assured him this was normal.

4 *Lingering for Lunch* Noon

Fallingwater's inviting grounds, not to mention various vantage points for your perfect photo, will keep you busy until lunchtime, so stay for a sandwich at the cafe. The shopping is good, too. At the Fallingwater Museum Store, even the souvenir mugs are classy.

5 *A Bike in the Forest* 1 p.m.

In Confluence, a tiny, charming town wedged between the tines of three converging rivers, you'll find the gateway to the most beautiful 11 miles of the 150-mile **Great Allegheny Passage** rail trail (atatrail.org), following an old railroad bed. Rent a mountain bike or a recumbent (easy on the body if you're not a regular cyclist) from one of the village outfitters, and glide through the dreamy woodland of **Ohiopyle State Park** (dcnr.state.pa.us/stateparks/parks/ohiopyle.aspx).

6 *Nature's Water Park* 3 p.m.

Cool down in the **Natural Waterslides**, still in the park, just south of Ohiopyle on Route 381. Sit in the stream, and it barrels you across smooth rocks and through a curving sluice, producing an adrenaline rush and maybe a few bruises. Dry off by **Cucumber Falls** around the corner on Route 2019, a bridal veil that splashes into a pool the pale green and rusty red of a glass of Pimm's. When you feel refreshed, cycle back to Confluence and drop off your bike.

7 *Going Usonian* 7:30 p.m.

Make your way over hill and dale to secluded **Polymath Park** (187 Evergreen Lane, Acme; 877-833-7829; polymathpark.com), a quiet, tree-shaded resort whose intriguing business plan centers on architectural preservation. You made your dinner reservations here long ago, so take a little time now to explore the shaded drives and find the **Duncan House**, one of the modest houses that Frank Lloyd Wright designed for the middle class and christened Usonians. Rescued from its original site in Illinois, where it was threatened with teardown, it was moved

to Pennsylvania in thousands of numbered pieces and, after some cliffhanger misadventures, painstakingly reassembled here. The house is vastly more modest than the tour de force of Fallingwater, but it bears the unmistakable marks of Wright's ingenuity. It is available for short-term rentals, so be respectful of the tenants who may be inside and view it from a distance. (Unless, of course, you are the lucky tenant this weekend yourself, in which case you are already well into a uniquely memorable experience.) Wind along the other drives to find three more houses, designed by Wright apprentices and also available as lodging.

8 *Food of the Polymaths* 8 p.m.

The fare runs to entrees like pecan-crusted brook trout and wood-fired filet mignon at **Tree Tops Restaurant** (877-833-7829; $$-$$$) on the Polymath Park grounds. Soak in the atmosphere and share the evening with the other Wright groupies who will have found their way to this quiet spot. If the night is right, you can exchange some stories.

SUNDAY

9 *His Lordship's Getaway* 10 a.m.

Kentuck Knob (723 Kentuck Road, Chalk Hill; 724-329-1901; kentuckknob.com), in another wooded setting, represents the middle ground of your Wright

OPPOSITE ABOVE AND RIGHT **OPPOSITE ABOVE AND RIGHT** Wright's Duncan House, re-assembled in Polymath Park after facing destruction on its original site in Lisle, Illinois, is available for short-term stays.

OPPOSITE BELOW A swivel gun demonstration at Fort Necessity National Battlefield, where Colonel George Washington, just 22 years old, surrendered to the enemy in a battle of the French and Indian War.

weekend: far less spectacular than Fallingwater, but far more so than the Duncan House. A stone-and-cypress hexagon with a balcony ending in a stone prow, it is full of eccentric angles and unexpected viewpoints that add up to the usual Wrightian mastery. Wright designed it as a hillside home for a local ice cream magnate, but the current owner is a British lord who not only lets the public traipse through but also displays his collectibles, from

Claes Oldenburg sculptures to bullets from Custer's Last Stand. Take the tour and then take your time on the grounds.

10 *Tuck It In* 1 p.m.

Locals praise the food at the **Out of the Fire Cafe** (3784 State Route 31, Donegal; 724-593-4200; outofthefirecafe.com; $$), and it's a good spot for a substantial Sunday dinner: an apple-stuffed pork chop with garlic potatoes, perhaps, or pan-seared Scottish salmon with sweet potato and roasted corn hash. Tuck it away, and it should get you all the way back home.

THE BASICS

The Laurel Highlands are southeast of Pittsburgh. The country roads can be confusing. Arm yourself with maps, a GPS unit, and a cellphone.

The Duncan House
187 Evergreen Lane, Acme
877-833-7829
polymathpark.com
$$$$
Designed by Frank Lloyd Wright. Stay overnight and pretend he built it just for you.

Summit Inn Resort
101 Skyline Drive, Farmington
724-438-8594
summitinnresort.com
$$
Porch rockers and mountain views.

Hampton Inn Uniontown
698 West Main Street, Uniontown
724-430-1000
hamptoninn.com
$$
One of several chain options.

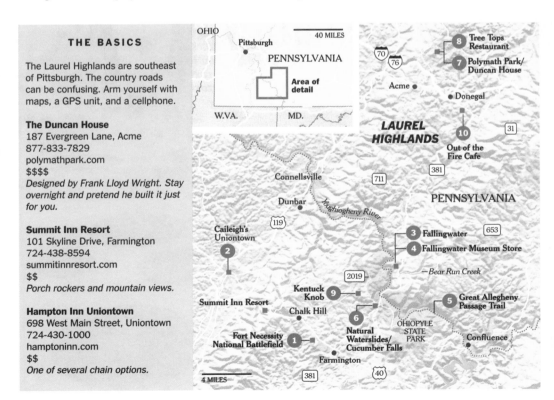

Pittsburgh

Pittsburgh has undergone a striking renaissance from a down-and-out smokestack town to a gleaming cultural oasis known for educational and technical prowess. There are great restaurants, excellent shopping, breakthrough galleries, and prestigious museums. The convergence of three rivers and surrounding green hills make a surprisingly pretty urban setting, and with abandoned steel mills long since torn down, more of the natural beauty of this part of Pennsylvania has emerged. If the Pirates are in town, head to the waterfront ballpark. Besides seeing the game, you'll have an excuse to explore downtown and take in the river views.
— BY JEFF SCHLEGEL

FRIDAY

1 *Gridiron and Steel* 4 p.m.

Get to know what makes the city tick at the **Senator John Heinz History Center** (1212 Smallman Street; 412-454-6000; pghhistory.org), which chronicles past and present glories from United States Steel to the Pittsburgh Steelers. This is actually a twofer: the main museum is devoted to everything from the Heinz food empire to the city's polyglot population. The upper two floors are occupied by the Western Pennsylvania Sports Museum.

2 *Waterfall Dining* 7 p.m.

The martini menu changes almost as often at the seasonal specials at **Soba** (5847 Ellsworth Avenue; 412-362-5656; bigburrito.com/soba; $$$), a pan-Asian restaurant with a Victorian exterior and a Zen-like interior that features a two-story wall of cascading water. Scan the menu for dishes like lobster maki and seafood and tandoori-grilled salmon. The wine list is extensive, and the vibe is upscale and trendy, but not in an overbearing way. If you arrive early, grab a special martini, perhaps made with ginger-infused vodka, on the rooftop deck.

3 *Brillo Pad* 10 p.m.

Brillobox (4104 Penn Avenue; 412-621-4900; brillobox.net) feels like an arty bar in New York's East Village — little wonder, considering the 30-something artist couple who own it are former New Yorkers. They came back home to Pittsburgh, they

said, to contribute to the city's growing arts scene, and if the name of their establishment reminds you of Andy Warhol, you're on the right track. Pittsburgh is Warhol's hometown, and the Andy Warhol Museum Downtown holds 12,000 of his works. Brillobox catches some of his adventurous spirit with art film screenings, spoken-word performances, and live music held upstairs in a room decked out in velvet wallpaper and murals. But you can just hang loose in the downstairs bar with its atmospheric red lights and an eclectic jukebox that has Goldfrapp, Patsy Cline, and Snoop Dogg.

SATURDAY

4 *Nosh 'n' Stroll* 10:30 a.m.

By night, the formerly industrial **Strip District** is filled with partygoers bouncing between bars and clubs. But on Saturday mornings, the parallel thoroughfares of Penn Avenue and Smallman Street (roughly between 16th and 26th Streets) are turned into a sprawling outdoor market with international food kiosks that serve Middle Eastern kebabs, Italian sausages, and Greek baklava. Shop for produce, clothing, and vintage knickknacks as accordionists and mariachi bands provide a festive soundtrack. Take a breather with a cup of coffee and a mele, a

OPPOSITE The Mattress Factory on the North Side, home to room-size installations from artists like Yayoi Kusama.

BELOW The Duquesne Incline, a funicular first opened in 1877, takes passengers to Mount Washington for a view of the city.

fruit-filled pastry, at **La Prima Espresso Bar** (205 21st Street; 412-281-1922; laprima.com), where the old men sitting at the outdoor tables look like they've been sipping espresso and playing cards for eternity.

5 *No Beds Here* 1 p.m.

If you're a Warhol fan, don't miss the **Andy Warhol Museum** (117 Sandusky Street; 412-237-8300; warhol.org). For more radical contemporary art, beat a new path in the Mexican War Streets neighborhood to the **Mattress Factory** (500 Sampsonia Way; 412-231-3169; mattress.org). Housed in a former mattress factory, the museum is dedicated to room-size art installations.

6 *Hard-to-Find Items* 3 p.m.

Some of the city's funkiest shopping can be found in the **16:62 Design Zone** (1662designzone.com), which spans the Strip District and Lawrenceville neighborhoods. It has more than 100 locally owned shops that focus on design, home décor, contemporary art, clothing, and architecture. Among the more interesting is the nonprofit **Society for Contemporary Craft** (2100 Smallman Street; 412-261-7003; contemporarycraft.org), a gallery and store that showcases handmade crafts like shiny metal handbags ($300 to $500) and recycled steel cabinets (from $3,500).

7 *Grab the Camera* 6 p.m.

The best views of Pittsburgh are from Mount Washington, and the best way to get there—or at least the most fun—is up the **Duquesne Incline** (1220 Grandview Avenue; 412-381-1665; incline.cc). One of two surviving hillside cable cars from the 1870s, it takes three minutes to climb 800 feet to Grandview

ABOVE Andy Warhol was from Pittsburgh, and thousands of his works have come to his namesake museum.

RIGHT A table with a view at the Monterey Bay Fish Grotto on Grandview's restaurant row.

Avenue. There's a neat little history museum at the top that has old newspaper clippings, but the real spectacle is the view of downtown Pittsburgh, where the Allegheny and Monongahela Rivers meet to form the Ohio.

8 *City Under Glass* 7 p.m.

While you're up there, Grandview Avenue is also home to a cliff-hugging restaurant row. For amazing seafood to go with the river views, make reservations for the **Monterey Bay Fish Grotto** (1411 Grandview Avenue; 412-481-4414; montereybayfishgrotto.com; $$$). This tri-level restaurant sits atop a 10-story apartment building. Jackets aren't required, but nice clothes are apropos. Fresh fish is flown in daily, and the menu changes often. On one visit the specials included a charcoal-grilled Atlantic salmon with fresh peppered strawberries in a red-wine sauce.

9 *Off-Downtown Theater* 9 p.m.

Generally regarded as Pittsburgh's most innovative theater company, the **City Theatre** (1300 Bingham Street; 412-431-2489; citytheatrecompany.org) does challenging plays that aren't likely to be staged in the downtown cultural district. Housed in a pair of former churches, it has both a 272-seat mainstage and a more intimate 110-seat theater. After the show, stop in at **Dee's Cafe** (1314 East Carson Street; 412-431-1314;

deescafe.com), a comfortable, jam-packed dive that is part of what by some counts is the country's longest continuous stretch of bars.

SUNDAY

10 *Brunch and Bric-a-Brac* 11 a.m.

One of city's more unusual brunch spots is the **Zenith** (86 South 26th Street; 412-481-4833; zenithpgh.com; $-$$), a combination art gallery, vintage clothing store, antiques shop, and vegetarian restaurant. For those who can't stomach tofu, brunch includes traditional staples like eggs, pancakes, and French toast. It gets busy, so to avoid the line, get there before it opens at 11.

11 *Brain Food* 12:30 p.m.

The Oakland district teems with intellectual energy from the University of Pittsburgh, Carnegie Mellon University, and several museums. Start out at the Nationality Rooms at the **Cathedral of Learning** (4200 Fifth Avenue; 412-624-6000; pitt.edu/~natrooms), a 42-story Gothic-style tower on the Pittsburgh campus with 27 classrooms, each devoted to a different nationality. Then head over to the renowned **Carnegie Museum of Art** (412-622-3131; cmoa.org) and **Carnegie Natural History Museum** (carnegiemnh.org), both at 4400 Forbes Avenue, for Degas and dinosaurs. Before leaving, pick up a handy walking tour of Oakland and public art in the neighborhood.

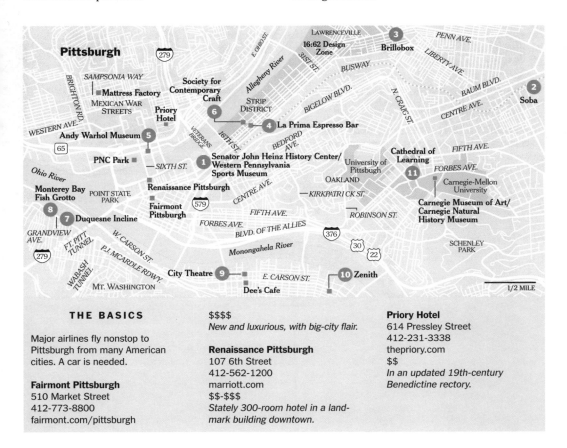

THE BASICS

Major airlines fly nonstop to Pittsburgh from many American cities. A car is needed.

Fairmont Pittsburgh
510 Market Street
412-773-8800
fairmont.com/pittsburgh

$$$$
New and luxurious, with big-city flair.

Renaissance Pittsburgh
107 6th Street
412-562-1200
marriott.com
$$-$$$
Stately 300-room hotel in a landmark building downtown.

Priory Hotel
614 Pressley Street
412-231-3338
thepriory.com
$$
In an updated 19th-century Benedictine rectory.

Cleveland

"You Gotta Be Tough" was a popular T-shirt slogan worn by Clevelanders during the 1970s, a grim period marked by industrial decline, large-scale population flight, and an urban environment so toxic that the Cuyahoga River actually caught on fire. These days it still helps to be at least a little tough; a fiercely blue-collar ethos endures in this part of Ohio. But instead of abandoning the city, local entrepreneurs and bohemian dreamers alike are sinking roots; opening a wave of funky boutiques, offbeat art galleries, and sophisticated restaurants; and injecting fresh life into previously rusted-out spaces. Spend the weekend and catch the vibrant spirit. — BRETT SOKOL

FRIDAY

1 *Hello, Cleveland!* 3 p.m.

Staring at platform shoes worn by Keith Moon or at Elvis Presley's white jumpsuit hardly evokes the visceral excitement of rock music, let alone its rich history, but the **Rock and Roll Hall of Fame and Museum** (751 Erieside Avenue; 216-781-7625; rockhall.com) has a wealth of interactive exhibits in addition to its displays of the goofier fashion choices of rock stardom. There's a fascinating look at the genre's initial 1950s heyday, as well as the hysteria that greeted it — preachers and politicians warning of everything from incipient Communist subversion to wanton sexuality.

2 *Iron Chef, Polish Comfort* 7 p.m.

Cleveland's restaurant of popular distinction is **Lolita** (900 Literary Road; 216-771-5652; lolabistro.com; $$$), where the owner, *Iron Chef America* regular Michael Symon, offers creative spins on Mediterranean favorites like duck prosciutto pizza and crispy chicken livers with polenta, wild mushrooms, and pancetta. (Reservations are recommended.) More traditional comfort food is at **Sokolowski's University Inn** (1201 University Road; 216-771-9236; sokolowskis.com; $), a beloved stop for classic Polish dishes since 1923.

OPPOSITE The Cleveland Museum of Art in the culture-saturated University Circle district.

RIGHT At the Velvet Tango Room, the bitters are house-made and the cocktails are precisely mixed.

Even if you're unswayed by Anthony Bourdain's description of the smoked kielbasa as "artery busting" (from him, a compliment) at least swing by for the view from the parking lot — a panorama encompassing Cleveland old and new, from the stadiums dotting the downtown skyline to the smoking factories and oddly beautiful slag heaps on the riverside below.

3 *Classic Cocktails* 10 p.m.

Discerning drinkers head for the **Velvet Tango Room** (2095 Columbus Road; 216-241-8869; velvettangoroom.com), inside a one-time Prohibition-era speakeasy and seemingly little changed: the bitters are house-made, and the bartenders pride themselves on effortlessly mixing a perfect Bourbon Daisy or Rangpur Gimlet. Yes, as their menu explains, you can order a chocolate-tini — "But we die a little bit every time."

SATURDAY

4 *Farm-Fresh* 10 a.m.

Start your day at the **West Side Market** (1979 West 25th Street; 216-664-3387; westsidemarket.com), where many of the city's chefs go to stock their own kitchens. Browse over stalls where 100 vendors sell meat, cheese, fruit, vegetables, and baked goods, or just pull up a chair at **Crêpes De Luxe**'s counter (crepesdeluxe.com; $) for a savory Montréal (filled with smoked brisket and Emmental cheese) or the Elvis homage Le Roi (bananas, peanut butter, and chocolate).

5 *From Steel to Stylish* Noon

The steelworkers who once filled the Tremont neighborhood's low-slung houses and ornately topped churches have largely vanished. A new breed of resident has moved in along with a wealth of upscale restaurants, galleries, and artisanal shops. Inside **Lilly Handmade Chocolates** (761 Starkweather Avenue; 216-771-3333; lillytremont.com), you can join the throngs practically drooling over the mounds of freshly made truffles. Or grab a glass at the wine bar inside **Visible Voice Books** (1023 Kenilworth Avenue; 216-961-0084; visiblevoicebooks.com), which features scores of small-press titles, many by local authors.

6 *Some Still Like Canvas* 3 p.m.

For more than 20 years the **William Busta Gallery** (2731 Prospect Avenue; 216-298-9071; williambustagallery.com) has remained a conceptual-art-free zone — video installations included. "With video, it takes 15 minutes to see how bad somebody really is," said Mr. Busta, the gallery's owner. "With painting, you can spot talent right away." And that's predominantly what he exhibits, with a focus on exciting homegrown figures like Don Harvey and Matthew Kolodziej. In the nearby Warehouse District, **Shaheen Modern & Contemporary Art** (740 West Superior Avenue, Suite 101; 216-830-8888; shaheengallery.com) casts a wider geographic net with solo exhibits from New York-based artists.

7 *Paris on Lake Erie* 6 p.m.

A much talked-about spot is **L'Albatros** (11401 Bellflower Road; 216-791-7880; albatrosbrasserie.com; $$), run by the chef Zachary Bruell. Set inside a 19th-century carriage house on the campus of Case Western Reserve University, this inviting brasserie serves impeccably executed French specialties like chicken liver and foie gras mousseline, a niçoise salad, and cassoulet.

8 *Ballroom Blitz* 8 p.m.

The polka bands are long gone from the **Beachland Ballroom** (15711 Waterloo Road; 216-383-1124; beachlandballroom.com), replaced by an eclectic mix of rock groups. But by running a place that's as much a clubhouse as a concert venue, the co-owners Cindy Barber and Mark Leddy have retained plenty of this former Croatian social hall's old-school character. Beachland books national bands and favorite local acts. Mr. Leddy, formerly an antiques dealer, still hunts down finds for the This Way Out Vintage Shoppe in the basement.

ABOVE The Rock and Roll Hall of Fame, repository of John Lennon's "Sgt. Pepper" suit and Michael Jackson's glove.

BELOW Home cooks and chefs both stock their kitchens at the West Side Market, a good stop for Saturday morning.

SUNDAY

9 *Beets, Then Beats* 10 a.m.

One of the few restaurants in town where requesting the vegan option won't elicit a raised eyebrow, **Tommy's** (1824 Coventry Road; 216-321-7757; tommyscoventry.com; $) has been serving tofu since 1972, when the surrounding Coventry Village, in Cleveland Heights, was a hippie oasis. The bloom is off that countercultural rose, but the delicious falafel and thick milkshakes endure. The time warp continues through a doorway leading into **Mac's Backs** bookstore (No. 1820; 216-321-2665; macsbacks.com), a good place to find out-of-print poetry from Cleveland post-Beat writers like d.a. levy, T. L. Kryss, and rjs.

10 *Free Impressionists* Noon

For decades, the University Circle district has housed many of the city's cultural jewels, including Severance Hall, the majestic Georgian residence of the Cleveland Orchestra; the Cleveland Institute of Art Cinematheque, one of the country's best repertory movie theaters; and the lush 285-acre Lake View Cemetery. At the **Cleveland Museum of Art** (11150 East Boulevard; 216-421-7340; clemusart.com), already famed for its collection of Old Masters and kid-friendly armor, the opening of the Rafael Viñoly-designed East Wing has put the spotlight on more modern fare, from one of Monet's Water Lilies paintings to current work. A further enticement: admission to the museum's permanent collection is absolutely free.

THE BASICS

Several major airlines have frequent flights to Cleveland. A light rail system connects the airport with downtown and University Circle. A car is needed for reaching most other neighborhoods.

The Glidden House
1901 Ford Drive
866-812-4537
gliddenhouse.com
$$
Quaint rooms in a 1910 mansion on the Case Western Reserve University campus.

Renaissance Cleveland Hotel
24 Public Square
216-696-5600
marriott.com
$$-$$$
A renovated elegant downtown classic, now a Marriott property.

Marriott Downtown at Key Center
127 Public Square
216-696-9200
marriott.com
$$-$$$
Some rooms with lake views.

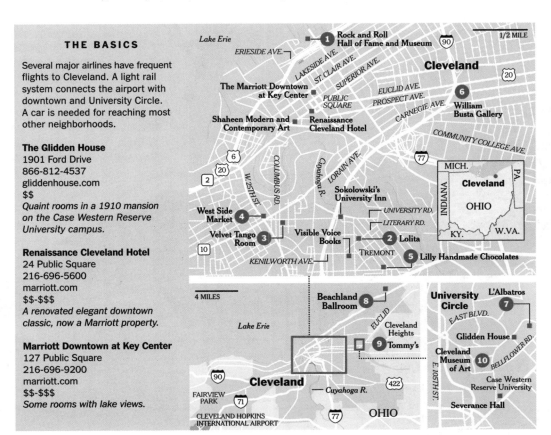

Cincinnati

With the quiet momentum of a work in progress, Cincinnati, Ohio, is finding an artsy swagger, infused with a casual combination of Midwest and Southern charm. The city center, for decades rich with cultural and performing arts venues, now offers a renovated Fountain Square area and a gleaming new baseball stadium with views of the Ohio River. Transformations are taking place in surrounding areas and across the river in the neighboring Kentucky cities of Newport and Covington—with cool music venues, funky shopping outlets, and smart culinary options. While it looks to the future, the city also honors its historic role in the antislavery movement with its National Underground Railroad Freedom Center. — BY KASSIE BRACKEN

FRIDAY

1 *Tranquility and Eternity* 4 p.m.

A graveyard may not be the most obvious place to start a trip, but **Spring Grove Cemetery and Arboretum** (4521 Spring Grove Avenue; 513-681-7526; springgrove.org/sg/arboretum/arboretum.shtm) is not your average resting place. The arboretum, designed in 1845 as a place for botanical experiments, features 1,200 types of plants artfully arranged around mausoleums and tranquil ponds. Roman- and Greek-inspired monuments bear the names of many of Cincinnati's most prominent families, including the Procters and the Gambles, whose business, begun in the 1830s, still dominates Cincinnati. Admission and parking are free, and the office provides printed guides and information about the plant collection.

2 *Where Hipsters Roam* 6 p.m.

The Northside district has blossomed into a casually hip destination for shopping and night life, particularly along Hamilton Avenue. Vinyl gets ample real estate at **Shake It Records** (4156 Hamilton Avenue; 513-591-0123; shakeitrecords.com), a music store specializing in independent labels; if you can't find a title among the 40,000 they carry, the owners will track it down for you. For a bite, locals swear by **Melt**

OPPOSITE The John A. Roebling Suspension Bridge over the Ohio River connects Cincinnati to its Kentucky suburbs.

RIGHT The revitalized Over-the-Rhine neighborhood.

Eclectic Deli (4165 Hamilton Avenue; 513-681-6358; meltcincy.com; $), a quirky restaurant friendly to vegans and carnivores alike. Order the Joan of Arc sandwich, with blue cheese and caramelized onions atop roast beef, or the hummus-laden Helen of Troy, and retreat to the patio.

3 *Local Bands, Local Beer* 9 p.m.

Saunter next door to find 20-somethings in skinny jeans mingling with 30-somethings in flip-flops at **Northside Tavern** (4163 Hamilton Avenue; 513-542-3603; northside-tavern.com), a prime spot for live music. Sip a pint of Cincinnati's own Christian Moerlein beer and listen to jazz, blues, and acoustic rock acts in the intimate front bar. Or head to the back room, where the best local bands take the larger stage. Wind down with a crowd heavy with artists and musicians at the **Comet** (4579 Hamilton Avenue; 513-541-8900; cometbar.com), a noirish dive bar with an impossibly cool selection on its jukebox and top-notch burritos to satisfy any late-night cravings.

SATURDAY

4 *The Aerobic Arabesque* 9:30 a.m.

The fiberglass pigs in tutus that greet you outside the **Cincinnati Ballet** (1555 Central Parkway; 513-621-5219) might indicate otherwise, but don't be fooled: the Ballet's Open Adult Division program (cballet.org/academy/adult) is a great place to get lean. Start your Saturday with a beginning ballet class (90 minutes, under $20), as a company member steers novices through basic movements. More experienced dancers might try the one-hour Rhythm

and Motion class, which combines hip-hop, modern, and African dance. Regulars know the moves, so pick a spot in the back and prepare to sweat.

5 *A Bridge to Brunch* 11:30 a.m.

If John Roebling's Suspension Bridge looks familiar, you might be thinking of his more famous design in New York. (Cincinnati's version opened in 1867, almost two decades before the Brooklyn Bridge.) It's a pedestrian-friendly span over the Ohio River, providing terrific views of the skyline. Cross into Covington, Kentucky, and walk a few blocks to the **Keystone Bar & Grill** (313 Greenup Street; 859-261-6777; keystonebar.com; $-$$), where alcohol-fueled partying gives way to brunch on weekend mornings and the menu runs heavily to gravy. You'll be well fueled for the walk back.

6 *Tracing a Legacy* 2 p.m.

The **National Underground Railroad Freedom Center** (50 East Freedom Way; 513-333-7500; freedomcenter.org) is a dynamic testament to Cincinnati's place in the antislavery movement. Multimedia presentations, art displays, and interactive timelines trace the history of the global slave trade as well as 21st-century human trafficking. Leave time for the genealogy center, where volunteers assist individuals with detailed family searches.

7 *Sin City, Updated* 5 p.m.

For decades, Cincinnatians scoffed at their Kentucky neighbors, but that has been changing in the last few years, especially with the revitalization of Newport, a waterfront and historic housing district. Stroll to **York St. Café** (738 York Street, entrance

on Eighth Street; 859-261-9675; yorkstonline.com; $$), an 1880s-era apothecary transformed into a three-story restaurant, music, and art space, where wood shelves are stocked with kitschy memorabilia. Browse a bit before scanning the menu for bistro fare like a Mediterranean board (an array of shareable appetizers) or a delicate fresh halibut with spinach and artichoke. Leave room for the excellent homemade desserts, including the strawberry buttermilk cake.

8 *Stage to Stage* 7 p.m.

Cincinnati Playhouse in the Park (962 Mount Adams Circle; 513-421-3888; cincyplay.com), which has been producing plays for five decades, offers splendid vistas of Mount Adams and a solid theatergoing experience. A lesser-known but equally engaging option can be found at the **University of Cincinnati College-Conservatory of Music** (Corry Boulevard; 513-556-4183; ccm.uc.edu/theatre). Students dreaming of Lincoln Center perform in full-scale productions of serious drama and opera. Check the online calendar for showtimes and locations.

9 *Ballroom Bliss* 10 p.m.

Head back to Newport's Third Street and its bars and clubs. A standout, **Southgate House**, is set in an 1814 Victorian mansion that resembles a haunted fraternity (24 East Third Street, Newport; 859-431-2201; southgatehouse.com). It hosts local and national acts dabbling in everything from bluegrass to death metal. On a typical Saturday night, music fans of all ages and sensibilities roam the three venues: an intimate parlor room, a laid-back lounge, and a ballroom with a capacity of 600.

ABOVE Spring Grove Cemetery and Arboretum.

RIGHT Northside, an area for shopping and night life.

OPPOSITE The National Underground Railroad Freedom Center. Cincinnati was a stop for many who escaped slavery.

SUNDAY

10 *Neighborhood Reborn* 10 a.m.

As the epicenter of 19th-century German immigrant society, the neighborhood known as Over-the-Rhine once teemed with breweries, theaters, and social halls. Though it fell into disrepair and parts remain rough around the edges, an $80 million revitalization effort has slowly brought back visitors. Walk down Main Street between 12th and 15th Streets to find local artists' galleries and the **Iris BookCafe** (1331 Main Street; 513-381-2665), a serene rare-book shop with an outdoor sculpture garden. A few blocks away, Vine Street between Central Parkway and 13th Street offers new boutiques including the craft shop **MiCA 12/v** (1201 Vine Street; 513-421-3500; shopmica.com), which specializes in

contemporary designers like Jonathan Adler and Kenneth Wingard.

11 *Designs to Take Home* 1 p.m.

Before heading home, find inspiring décor at **HighStreet** (1401 Reading Road; 513-723-1901; highstreetcincinnati.com), a spacious and sleek design store. The owners have carefully composed a cosmopolitan mix of textiles, clothing, and jewelry by New York and London designers as well as local artists, showcased in a creatively appointed space. A free cup of red flower tea makes it all the more inviting.

THE BASICS

Fly into Cincinnati/Northern Kentucky International Airport, a 25-minute drive from downtown. A rental car is recommended.

Hilton Cincinnati Netherland Plaza
35 West Fifth Street
513-421-9100
hilton.com
$$
561 renovated rooms in a landmark building, the Art Deco Carew Tower.

The Westin Cincinnati
21 East Fifth Street
513-621-7700
starwoodhotels.com
$$
Downtown with views of Fountain Square from many rooms.

Cincinnatian Hotel
601 Vine Street
513-381-3000
cincinnatianhotel.com
$$
Updated rooms in a classic hotel dating to 1882.

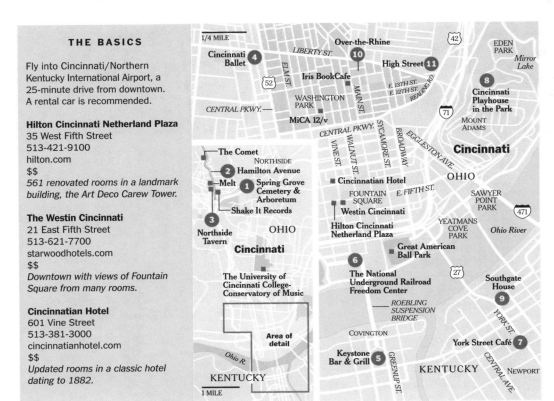

Indianapolis

For years, Indianapolis, Indiana, bore the stigma of nicknames like Nap Town and Indiana No Place. But then construction and development downtown seemed to wake the city up, and today, a thriving cultural scene and the multiethnic influences of immigrant populations mix with Hoosier hospitality and charm. And there are still the old Indianapolis standbys, like the hearty Midwestern food; the many classical monuments and fountains, laid out using elements of Pierre L'Enfant's plan for Washington and built partly by Freemasons; and of course, the Indianapolis Motor Speedway, home of the Indy 500. — BY JOHN HOLL

FRIDAY

1 *A Cocktail with That Scotch* 6:30 p.m.

Start with a drink downtown at one of the city's oldest restaurants, **St. Elmo Steak House** (127 South Illinois Street; 317-635-0636; stelmos.com; $$$), where for more than a century patrons have sidled up to the tiger oak bar—first used in the 1893 Chicago World's Fair—for martinis and single malts. Settle in under the gaze of the Indiana celebrities whose photos adorn the walls (David Letterman, Larry Bird) and try St. Elmo's not-for-the-faint-of-heart signature dish: the shrimp cocktail. The jumbo shrimp are served smothered in horseradish cocktail sauce made every hour to ensure freshness and a proper sinus assault. If you can see through the tears in your eyes, you'll probably notice one of the tuxedoed bartenders having a quiet chuckle at your expense.

2 *New Indiana* 7 p.m.

While downtown has been rejuvenating itself with new development, areas out toward the suburbs have been transformed by immigration, with Pakistanis, Salvadorans, Burmese, and an assortment of other groups mingling comfortably. To see a bit of what this melting pot has brought to Indianapolis dining, drive a few miles to **Abyssinia** (5352 West 38th Street, in the Honey Creek Plaza; 317-299-0608; $), an Ethiopian restaurant decorated with Haile Selassie portraits

OPPOSITE The Canal Walk in downtown Indianapolis.

RIGHT Take the dare and order the super-spicy horseradish shrimp cocktail at the century-old St. Elmo Steak House.

and Ethiopia tourism posters. The authentic, well-cooked cuisine incorporates lots of lentils as well as goat in berbere sauce, house-made injera bread, and sambusas, the Ethiopian version of samosas. The place draws Africans, Indians, vegans, and plenty of longtime Indianans who like a culinary adventure.

3 *Blues and Bands* 10:30 p.m.

Indianapolis has had a blues scene for generations, and it's still alive and kickin' at the **Slippery Noodle Inn** (372 South Meridian Street; 317-631-6974; slipperynoodle.com). Housed in a two-story building constructed as a bar and roadhouse around 1850, the Noodle attracts a lively crowd (including, back in the day, the Dillinger Gang) and nationally known blues musicians like Country Joe McDonald and Ronnie Earl. But it's the local bands that make the place rock, so hoist a pint of the Indiana-brewed Upland IPA and groove on the dance floor to the thumping bass.

SATURDAY

4 *Monumental Efforts* 10 a.m.

Start a walking tour in the heart of downtown at the neoclassical **Soldiers and Sailors Monument** (1 Monument Circle; 317-232-7615), a 284-foot tall obelisk dating back to 1902. Look over the Civil War museum in the base and then take the elevator or brave the 330 stairs to the top. Back on the ground, it's a short walk down West Market Street to the **Indiana Statehouse**, a suitably domed and columned structure built in 1888.

A few blocks north is the **Freemasons' Scottish Rite Cathedral** (650 North Meridian Street; 800-489-3579; aasr-indy.org), actually a meeting hall, not a church. It's a tour de force of ornate decoration with a 212-foot tower, 54 bells, a 2,500-pound gilded bronze chandelier, cavernous oak-paneled halls, and stained-glass windows. If it's open (Monday through Friday and the third Saturday of each month), take an hourlong guided tour.

5 *Duckpins* Noon

Order a salad to keep it light at the **Smokehouse on Shelby** (317-685-1959; $) in the 1928 **Fountain Square Theatre Building** (1105 Prospect Street; fountainsquareindy.com), so that you can follow up with a chocolate malt or a strawberry soda from the restored 1950s soda fountain, rescued from a defunct Woolworth's. Then rent a lane and some shoes at one of the two duckpin bowling alleys in the building. The one upstairs still uses the original 1930s equipment. Downstairs has 50s-vintage bowling.

6 *White River Junction* 3 p.m.

Stroll along the canal and through the green spaces of **White River State Park** (801 West Washington Street; 317-233-2434; inwhiteriver.wrsp.in.gov) on the city's west side. You can take your pick of several museums and the Indianapolis Zoo, but a more unusual destination here is the headquarters

of the National Collegiate Athletic Association. The **N.C.A.A. Hall of Champions** (317-916-4255; ncaahallofchampions.org) has displays on 23 men's and women's sports, a theater showing memorable college sports moments, and interactive simulators that take you on a virtual trip into a game.

7 *Hoosier Heartland* 6 p.m.

For a real taste of Hoosier country (Indianans wear the Hoosier nickname proudly), grab some hors d'oeuvres and a bottle of wine and drive about 40 minutes northeast of the city, past farmland and cornfields, till you come to **Bonge's Tavern** (9830 West 280 North, Perkinsville; 765-734-1625; bongestavern.com; $$), a country roadhouse that opened in 1934. The restaurant does not take reservations for fewer than 10 people, so arrive early and be ready to wait 90 minutes or more. Part of the Bonge's experience is chatting with other patrons while sitting on rocking chairs on the enclosed porch, maybe sharing some of the wine and snacks you so thoughtfully brought. Once inside, order the Perkinsville Pork, a juicy, pounded-flat, parmesan-crusted loin that is worth waiting for.

8 *Basketball Bar* 10 p.m.

High school basketball is practically a religion in Indiana, and there is no more famous team than the 1954 squad from small Milan High School. They won the statewide championship on a final shot by

Bobby Plump, who quickly became a folk hero. The story formed the basis for the 1986 film *Hoosiers*. Today, Plump and his family operate a bar, **Plump's Last Shot** (6416 Cornell Avenue; 317-257-5867; plumpslastshot.com), a hoops-memorabilia-filled hangout in the Broad Ripple neighborhood and the perfect place to catch a game on TV.

SUNDAY

9 *Start Your Engines* Noon

Naturally you want to get a look at the **Indianapolis Motor Speedway** (4790 West 16th Street; 317-492-6784; indianapolismotorspeedway.com), home of the Indianapolis 500. The **Hall of Fame Museum** within the

racetrack grounds displays vintage race cars, trophies, and more than two dozen cars that won the race, including the very first winner (in 1911), a Marmon Wasp. The narrated bus ride around the fabled oval may be the closest you ever come to racing in the old Brickyard, but unfortunately the driver never gets above 30 miles an hour. You will get up-close views of the famed racing pagoda, Gasoline Alley, and the last remaining strip of the track's original brick surface, 36 inches wide, which now serves as the start/finish line.

OPPOSITE The first winner of the Indianapolis 500, on display at the Indianapolis Motor Speedway.

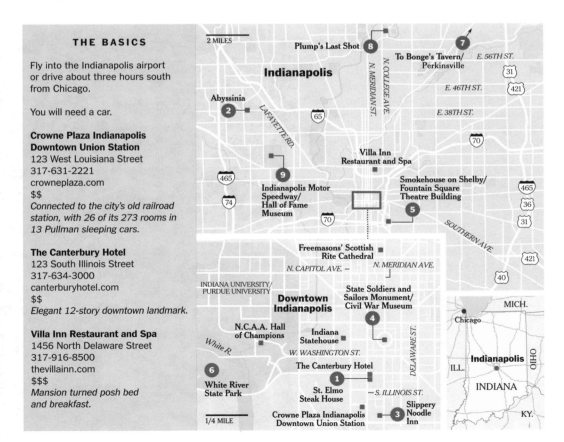

THE BASICS

Fly into the Indianapolis airport or drive about three hours south from Chicago.

You will need a car.

Crowne Plaza Indianapolis Downtown Union Station
123 West Louisiana Street
317-631-2221
crowneplaza.com
$$
Connected to the city's old railroad station, with 26 of its 273 rooms in 13 Pullman sleeping cars.

The Canterbury Hotel
123 South Illinois Street
317-634-3000
canterburyhotel.com
$$
Elegant 12-story downtown landmark.

Villa Inn Restaurant and Spa
1456 North Delaware Street
317-916-8500
thevillainn.com
$$$
Mansion turned posh bed and breakfast.

Iowa's Mississippi River

"For 60 years the foreign tourist has steamed up and down the river between St. Louis and New Orleans... believing he had seen all of the river that was worth seeing or that had anything to see," Mark Twain lamented in Life on the Mississippi. *The visitors were missing an "amazing region" to the north, he wrote. They were missing "extraordinary sunsets" and "enchanting scenery." They were missing Iowa. Today, tourists do find Iowa's Mississippi riverfront, thanks partly to modern confections like riverboat casinos and a water park resort, but much of this shore still feels undiscovered. Set out for a weekend car trip on quiet back roads, and you'll find the real life of the Mississippi amid green hilltops and fields, in small villages and busy cities, and on the wide river itself.*
— BY BETSY RUBINER

FRIDAY

1 *Skimming the River* 4 p.m.

Start your Mississippi River explorations in Davenport, about 1,775 miles upstream from the Gulf of Mexico. With no flood wall (though there are perennial arguments about whether to build one), downtown Davenport has a feeling of intimacy with the river, and you can get even closer on the **Channel Cat Water Taxi** (foot of Mound Street at the river; 309-788-3360; qcchannelcat.com) a small ferry with several stops. From its benches you may see blocks-long grain barges, speedboats, 19th-century riverbank mansions, or egrets on small wooded islands.

2 *Field of Dreams* 7 p.m.

One of the best points to enjoy Davenport's unusual eye-level river view is **Modern Woodmen Park** (209 South Gaines Street; 563-322-6348; riverbandits.com), the riverfront minor-league baseball field. If the River Bandits are playing at home, have some hot dogs or cheese steak as you take in a game. (There's also a tiki bar.) The park has a small cornfield where, when the stalks are

high enough, the Bandits emerge at game time like the ghostly players in *Field of Dreams*, which was filmed in Iowa. If it's not a game night, seek a more substantial dinner at **Front Street Brewery** (208 East River Drive; 563-322-1569; frontstreetbrew.com; $). Look on the menu for walleye, a favorite Midwestern native fish.

SATURDAY

3 *A River Still Traveled* 10 a.m.

Drive down to the levee at **Le Claire** to see a nicely preserved example of the craft used for traveling the river in Twain's day—the *Lone Star*, an 1860s sternwheel steamboat in dry dock at the **Buffalo Bill Museum** (199 North Front Street; 563-289-5580; buffalobillmuseumleclaire.com). Nearby, S.U.V.'s towing today's pleasure boats pull up to a launching ramp, disgorging day trippers toting kids, coolers, and life jackets. After the families have sped off, you may see them again, picnicking on an island. A block from the river, along Cody Road—named, as is the museum, for Le Claire's favorite son, William Cody—inviting shops and restaurants rejuvenate old brick storefronts.

4 *From the Heights* Noon

You're passing some of the world's most expensive farmland—fertile valley acreage conveniently close to river transportation on the grain barges—as you head north on Routes 67 and 52 to Bellevue. The town lives up to its name with sweeping views from the high bluffs at **Bellevue State Park** (24668 Highway 52; 563-872-4019; iowadnr.gov). A display in the park's

OPPOSITE Success in the form of a smallmouth bass, pulled from the Mississippi at McGregor.

RIGHT Try on a riverboat gambler's vest at the River Junction Trade Company, which makes Old West gear.

nature center recalls an early industry in these river towns: making buttons from mussel shells. In the pretty riverside downtown, check out the pizza at **2nd Street Station** (116 South 2nd Street; 563-872-5410) and stop for a look at **Lock and Dam No. 12** (Route 52 at Franklin Street). Locks are a common feature on the Upper Mississippi, where tugs push as many as 15 barges at a time, carrying as much freight as 870 tractor trailers or a 225-car train.

5 *Luxembourgers* 2:30 p.m.

Stop for a quick glance around tiny **St. Donatus**, where one of America's rarer ethnic groups, immigrants from Luxembourg, arrived in the 1800s and built limestone and stucco buildings. For some classic Iowa landscape (not waterscape), walk up the Way of the Cross path behind the Catholic church and look across the valley at patches of hay and corn quilting the hills. You may smell hogs. Or is it cattle?

6 *Gawk at the Gar* 3 p.m.

Spend some time in **Dubuque**, Davenport's rival Iowa river city. At the **National Mississippi River Museum and Aquarium** (350 East Third Street; 563-557-9545; rivermuseum.com), a Smithsonian affiliate, huge blue catfish, gar, and paddlefish swim in a 30,000-gallon tank, a boardwalk goes through reclaimed wetlands inhabited by herons and bald eagles, and a model shows havoc caused by a 1965

flood. Downtown, Dubuque feels like an old factory town, with Victorian mansions (several converted into inns), brick row houses flush to the street, and many a corner tap and church. Ride the **Fenelon Place Elevator** (512 Fenelon Place), a funicular that makes a steep climb to a bluff top where Wisconsin and Illinois are visible across the river.

7 *American Pie* 6 p.m.

Follow Highway 52 and the County Route C9Y, the Balltown Road, through a peaceful valley up and up onto a ridge with panoramic views worthy of a painting by Grant Wood (an Iowan): wide open sky, a lone pheasant in a field, alternating rows of crops, grazing cows, and tidy farms with stone houses, weathered red barns, and blue silos. Your goal is **Balltown**, which has 73 residents and one famous restaurant, **Breitbach's** (563 Balltown Road, Route C9Y; 563-552-2220; breitbachscountrydining.com; $-$$). It has been open since 1852 and is justly famed for its fried chicken, barbecued ribs, and fresh pie.

ABOVE Riverside baseball in Davenport.

OPPOSITE ABOVE The Fenelon Place Elevator in Dubuque climbs a steep bluff to a panoramic river view.

OPPOSITE BELOW Lock and Dam No. 12 spanning the river at Bellevue.

SUNDAY

8 *A "T" Too Far* 10 a.m.

Forty miles north of Dubuque, Highway 52 brings you to the river at **Guttenberg**, a lovely town settled by German immigrants in the 1840s and named after the inventor of moveable type, Johannes Gutenberg. (Word has it that an early typographical error accounts for the extra T.) Admire the downtown's well-preserved pre-Civil War-era limestone buildings and stroll at mile-long **Ingleside Park**. A few miles farther on, stop at **McGregor**, where boaters hang out by the marina and locals eat bratwurst and drink beer on riverview restaurant decks. Try on a riverboat gambler's vest or a feathered Victorian hat at the **River Junction Trade Company** (312 Main Street, McGregor; 866-259-9172; riverjunction.com), which makes reproductions of Old West gear, sometimes selling to Hollywood production companies.

9 *Pike's Other Peak* 11 a.m.

Even if you're getting weary of river panoramas, stop at **Pikes Peak State Park** (32264 Pikes Peak Road, McGregor; 563-873-2341; iowadnr.gov) to see one from the highest bluff on the Mississippi. Like Pikes Peak in Colorado, this spot is named for the explorer Zebulon Pike. Scouting for federal fort locations in 1805, Pike thought this peak was an ideal spot, and although the fort ended up across the river in Wisconsin, you can understand his reasoning. Look out at a swirl of green forested islands and mud-brown river pools. To the north, suspension bridges connect to Wisconsin. To the south, the Wisconsin River empties out at the place where in 1673 the

explorers Jacques Marquette and Louis Joliet first saw the Mississippi.

10 *Mound Builders* 1 p.m.

At **Effigy Mounds National Monument** (151 Highway 76, Harpers Ferry; 563-873-3491; nps.gov/efmo), 2,526 acres of grounds are dotted with mysterious prehistoric burial and ceremonial mounds, some as old as 2,500 years. The Indians of the Upper Midwest built large numbers of mounds shaped

like animals, most often bears and birds that lived along the Mississippi. Why they were built and who was meant to see them — since the best views are from the sky — remains unknown. Take the two-mile Fire Point Trail up a 360-foot bluff, through forests and past mounds. At the top, a clearing reveals a Mississippi that seems wild — with forested banks and islands, a soupy marsh, and hawks soaring above a bluff — until out of nowhere a speedboat zips by, breaking the silence.

ABOVE A houseboat anchored near McGregor.

OPPOSITE Downtown McGregor, a promising stop for Mississippi River souvenir hunters.

THE BASICS

The Mississippi River is a three-hour drive west from Chicago. The Quad City International Airport serves Davenport.

Hotel Blackhawk
200 East 3rd Street, Davenport
563-322-5000
hotelblackhawk.com
$$
Stylishly decorated landmark hotel, reopened in 2010 after extensive renovation.

Hotel Julien Dubuque
563-556-4200
200 Main Street, Dubuque
hoteljuliendubuque.com
$$
Modern boutique decorating, pool, and spa in a hotel with history dating back to Lincoln's day.

The Landing
703 South River Park Drive, Guttenberg
563-252-1615
thelanding615.com
$
Rooms and suites in a renovated stone riverfront warehouse.

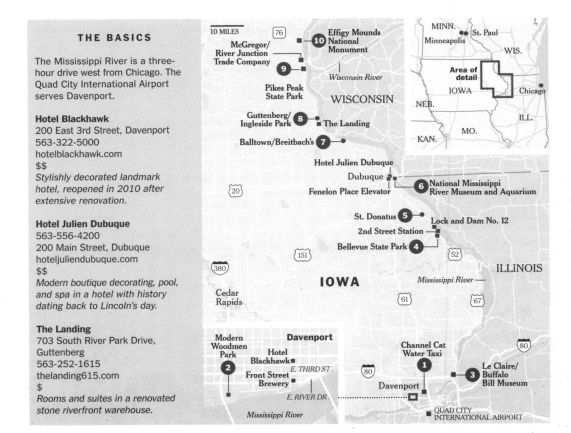

St. Louis

St. Louis, Missouri, is more than just a Gateway to the West. It's a lively destination in its own right, full of inviting neighborhoods, some coming out of a long decline and revitalized by public art, varied night life, and restaurants that draw on the bounty of surrounding farmland and rivers. The famous arch, of course, is still there, along with plenty of 19th-century architecture and an eye-opening amount of green space. Add to that a mix of Midwestern sensibility and Southern charm, and you've got plenty of reason to stay a while. — BY DAN SALTZSTEIN

FRIDAY

1 *Out in the Open* 4 p.m.

The new jewel of downtown St. Louis is **Citygarden** (citygardenstl.org), a sculpture park the city opened in 2009, framed by the old courthouse on one side and the Gateway Arch on the other. The oversize public art, by boldface-name artists like Mark di Suvero and Keith Haring, is terrific, but the real genius of the garden's layout is that it reflects the landscape of the St. Louis area: an arcing wall of local limestone, for instance, echoes the bends of the Mississippi and Missouri Rivers, which join just north of town.

2 *Up in the Sky* 6 p.m.

If you've never been to the top of the 630-foot **Gateway Arch** (gatewayarch.com), the four-minute ride up in a uniquely designed tram system is a must. And even if you have, it's worth reminding yourself that yes, that water down there is the Mississippi River, and that city spreading out beyond it is where a lot of optimistic Easterners slogged their first miles into the west. Eero Saarinen designed the arch, made of stainless steel, and it was completed in 1965. Besides providing a helicopter-height view, it's an elegantly simple artwork that endures.

3 *Soulard Soul* 8 p.m.

Historic Soulard (pronounced SOO-lard) is one of those neighborhoods experiencing a renaissance, thanks in part to several new quality restaurants. **Franco** (1535 South Eighth Street; 314-436-2500; eatatfranco.com; $$), an industrial-chic bistro that opened in 2007 next to the locally famous Soulard

farmers' market, serves soulful takes on French bistro fare, like country-fried frogs' legs in a red wine gravy and grilled Missouri rainbow trout in a crayfish and Cognac cream sauce.

4 *Analog Underground* 10 p.m.

Frederick's Music Lounge, a beloved St. Louis dive bar, is gone, but its legendary owner, Fred Boettcher Jr., a k a Fred Friction, has a new club beneath the restaurant Iron Barley. Follow signs for **FSFU — Fred's Six Feet Under** (5510 Virginia Avenue; 314-351-4500; ironbarley.com). Music venues don't get much more intimate; the band might take up a third of the total space. Drinks are cheap, and the tunes, courtesy of local bands like the Sins of the Pioneers, with their brand of New Orleans R&B, are as unpretentious as the crowd.

SATURDAY

5 *Cupcakes and Blooms* 9 a.m.

In the leafy neighborhood of Shaw, stately architecture mixes with hip spots like **SweetArt** (2203 South 39th Street; 314-771-4278; sweetartstl.com), a mom-and-pop bakery where you can eat a virtuous vegan breakfast topped off by a light-as-air cupcake.

OPPOSITE St. Louis's signature, the Gateway Arch designed by Eero Saarinen. Take the tram to the top, and you'll be riding up 630 feet on an elegant work of art.

BELOW The Missouri Botanical Garden.

Shaw is named for Henry Shaw, a botanist and philanthropist whose crowning achievement is the **Missouri Botanical Garden** (4344 Shaw Boulevard; 314-577-5100; mobot.org). Founded in 1859, it is billed as the oldest continuously operating botanical garden in the nation. It covers an impressive 79 acres and includes a large Japanese garden and Henry Shaw's 1850 estate home, as well as his (slightly creepy) mausoleum.

6 *Taste of Memphis* 1 p.m.

St. Louis-style ribs are found on menus across the country, but it's a Memphis-style joint (think slow-smoked meats, easy on the sauce) that seems to be the consensus favorite for barbecue in town. Just survey the best-of awards that decorate the walls at **Pappy's Smokehouse** (3106 Olive Street; 314-535-4340; pappyssmokehouse.com; $-$$). Crowds line up for heaping plates of meat and sides, served in an unassuming space (while you wait, take a peek at the smoker parked out back on a side street). The ribs and pulled pork are pretty good, but the winners might be the sides — bright and tangy slaw and deep-fried corn on the cob.

7 *Green Day* 3 p.m.

St. Louis boasts 105 city-run parks, but none rivals **Forest Park** (stlouis.missouri.org/citygov/parks/forestpark), which covers more than 1,200 acres smack in the heart of the city. It opened in 1876, but it was the 1904 World's Fair that made it a world-class public space, spawning comely buildings like the Palace of Fine Art, which now houses the Saint Louis Art Museum. In 2002, a $3.5 million renovation of the Jewel Box, a towering, contemporary-looking greenhouse dating back to 1936, gave it an extra sheen. Rent a bike from the visitor's center (314-367-7275; $35 a day) and just meander.

8 *Midwest Bounty* 8 p.m.

Locavore fever has hit St. Louis. Leading the pack may be **Local Harvest Cafe and Catering** (3137 Morgan Ford Road; 314-772-8815; localharvestcafe.com; $$$), a mellow spot in the Tower Grove neighborhood that's a spinoff of an organic grocery store across the street. A chalkboard menu lists all the local products featured that day, including items like honey and peanut butter. On Saturday nights the chef creates a four-course menu based on what's fresh at the farms and markets that morning. One menu included a light vegetarian cassoulet with beer pairings from local producers like Tin Mill Brewery.

9 *Royale Treatment* 10 p.m.

Tower Grove is also home to a handful of fine watering holes, including the **Royale** (3132 South Kingshighway Blvd.; 314-772-3600; theroyale.com), where an Art Deco-style bar of blond wood and glass is accompanied by old photos of political leaders (John F. Kennedy, Martin Luther King Jr., the late Missouri governor Mel Carnahan). But it's the extensive cocktail list, with drinks named after city neighborhoods (like the Carondelet Sazerac), and a backyard patio that keep the aficionados coming.

SUNDAY

10 *The Home Team* 10 a.m.

Take a number for one of the small, worn wooden tables at **Winslow's Home** (7211 Delmar Boulevard;

BELOW The Saint Louis Art Museum occupies a building from the 1904 World's Fair.

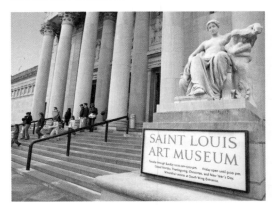

314-725-7559; winslowshome.com; $). It's more than just a pleasant place for brunch; it doubles as a general store that carries groceries, dry goods, and kitchen items like stainless steel olive oil dispensers. When it's time to order, try the brioche French toast with caramelized bananas. It's worth the wait.

11 *Art Class* Noon

Washington University gets high marks for its academics. But the campus, with its rolling green hills and grand halls, is also home to terrific contemporary art. See its collection at the **Mildred Lane Kemper Art Museum** (1 Brookings Drive; 314-935-4523; kemperartmuseum.wustl.edu). Designed by the Pritzker Prize-winning architect Fumihiko Maki, it's charmingly cramped and vaguely organized by theme — so you'll find a Jackson Pollock cheek

by jowl with a 19th-century portrait of Daniel Boone. You'll also find ambitious contemporary art exhibitions curated by Wash U faculty. Like much of St. Louis, the Kemper may not be flashy, but it's full of gems.

OPPOSITE ABOVE Oversize public art finds space at Citygarden, a downtown sculpture park.

ABOVE The extensive cocktail list at the Royale in the Tower Grove area features drinks — the Carondelet Sazerac, for one — that are named after city neighborhoods.

THE BASICS

Lambert International Airport is served by major airlines. For getting around in town, it's best to have a car.

Moonrise Hotel
6177 Delmar Boulevard
314-721-1111
moonrisehotel.com
$$
Pleasant boutique vibe and a central location.

Four Seasons St. Louis
999 North 2nd Street
314-881-5800
fourseasons.com/stlouis
$$$-$$$$
Part of a striking riverside complex that also includes a casino.

St. Louis Union Station Marriott
1820 Market Street
314-621-5262
www.marriott.com
$$
In the grand old downtown railroad station.

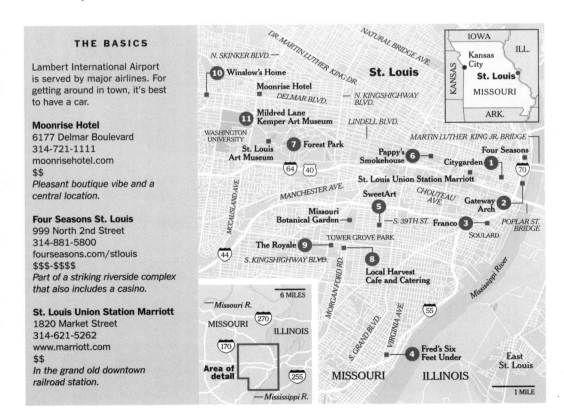

Fayetteville

A fast-growing college town in the Ozark foothills, Fayetteville, Arkansas, is flush with youth, character, and natural beauty — especially evident in spring, when the redbuds and dogwoods are in bloom. Hike the lush, forested trails that braid the area. Stroll through the leafy campus and holler "Wooooooooooo, Pig! Sooie!" at the 72,000-seat Reynolds Razorback Stadium at the University of Arkansas (but beware: hotels are probably already booked for the next football season). Soak up the atmosphere that entranced a young Bill Clinton. Then wind your way down lively Dickson Street, a former strip of dive bars that has gotten a good scrubbing. — BY JULIE BESONEN

FRIDAY

1 George's on My Mind 5:30 p.m.

Introspection is unthinkable at the boisterous **George's Majestic Lounge** (519 West Dickson Street; 479-442-4226; georgesmajesticlounge.com). Neither majestic nor a lounge, this wood-detailed beer garden with a retractable roof has anchored the Dickson Street music scene for four decades. There's always live music during the Friday happy hour. You might see the revered Cate Brothers, a soulful hometown band known for '70s hits like "Union Man," inspiring everyone to cut loose on the dance floor in broad daylight.

2 Notes from Underground 7 p.m.

Right off the late 19th-century town square is **Hugo's** (25 1/2 North Block Avenue; 479-521-7585; hugosfayetteville.com; $), a speakeasy-like basement bistro open since 1977 and overburdened with antique mirrors, vintage portraits, and commemorative presidential plates. Young families and spirited students aren't shy when it comes to tackling the juicy bleu-moon burger, catfish po' boy sandwich, baskets of fries, and homemade pecan pie. And there is a respectable beer selection as well.

3 Live from the Living Room 8 p.m.

When you're invited into someone's house for a concert and served coffee and cookies during intermission, it's a cozy, one-of-a-kind evening. Mike Shirkey, host of *The Pickin' Post* on KUAF public radio, frequently presents established folk

and bluegrass musicians, like Al and Emily Cantrell and Stacey Earle, on a stage in the club-size living room of an old wood-frame house very near Hugo's. Called **GoodFolk Productions** (229 North Block Avenue, 479-521-1812; goodfolk.org), it's almost as intimate as someone singing softly in your ear.

SATURDAY

4 Market on the Square 10 a.m.

Plenty of towns have farmers' markets, but the one looping around Fayetteville's **Downtown Square** (479-237-2910; fayettevillefarmersmarket.org) is uncommonly engaging. On one corner you might see a harpist and fiddler, on another a banjo player keeping time with a young country clogger whose hip attire and hairdo would not be out of place in Lower Manhattan. The homegrown produce for sale is not typical either: sheriff leeks, mediana spinach, and baby greens with edible flowers. Find the square at Block, Mountain, and Center Streets and East Avenue.

5 Young Love 11 a.m.

In 1975, on a salary of $16,450, Bill Clinton, a young University of Arkansas law professor, rashly bought a brick bungalow in Fayetteville for $20,500. Why? Because his elusive girlfriend, Hillary Rodham,

OPPOSITE The Tea Table Rocks in Ozark National Forest, east of Fayetteville.

BELOW The house where Bill and Hillary Clinton married and lived is now a museum with the wedding dress on view.

had made a passing remark on how pretty it was while he was driving her to the airport. When she returned to town, according to his autobiography, *My Life*, he said: "Remember that little house you liked so much? I bought it. You have to marry me now, because I can't live there alone." The ceremony was in the living room, and a reproduction of the bride's Victorian-style lace wedding dress is on display there today. So is early campaign memorabilia. The rest is history, and the house is now the **Clinton House Museum** (930 West Clinton Drive; 877-245-6445; clintonhousemuseum.org).

6 *Pick Up the Red Phone* 12:30 p.m.

Sink your teeth into the smoky, meaty, glazed rack of ribs at **Penguin Ed's B & B Bar-B-Q** (230 South East Avenue; 479-521-3663; penguineds.com; $$), and find rapture. Sides include fare like baked beans, home fries, and macaroni and cheese, but green vegetables are not unknown here. You can also get broccoli or a salad — even a garden burger. Penguin Ed's is in a cedar-lined shack with a tarred roof, and it has stuck with a tradition of having customers call in their orders from red phones at each table.

7 *Objets d'Ozark* 1:30 p.m.

Tired of traveling to regional arts-and-crafts shows to sell their work, several Ozark artists formed a collective and opened **Heartwood Gallery** (428 South Government Avenue; 479-444-0888; heartwoodgallery.org) several years ago. Imaginative jewelry, crazily colorful knit caps, striking watercolors, pottery, and handblown glass are some of the things you may be tempted to take home from the mountains.

ABOVE Hike rugged trails and explore caves at Devil's Den State Park, 25 miles south of Fayetteville.

RIGHT At the farmers' market, find the familiar and the unexpected: tulips and clog dancers, leeks and a harpist.

8 *Library Envy* 2 p.m.

You will need a card if you want to check out a book, but the **Fayetteville Public Library** (401 West Mountain Street; 479-571-2222; faylib.org) is worth checking out for its own sake. Through its sweeping windows you will find unparalleled views of the mountainous landscape. There's also free wireless, a cafe, a serene reading room, a genealogical collection, supercomfy chairs, and a lot of children's programs.

9 *Bivouac on a Mountainside* 4 p.m.

The only Confederate cemetery in Arkansas (500 East Rock Street) didn't open until 1873. The 622 well-ordered and mostly unmarked graves belong to Confederate soldiers who were originally buried where they fell, at nearby battlefields and roadsides or in lonely hollows. Eight years after the war ended, locals were paid $1.40 to $2.50 for each body exhumed and delivered for reburial. It was a tidy sum back then, and though most people probably took the task seriously, historians today are skeptical about some of the remains in the quiet glade on East Mountain.

10 *A Taste of Arkansas* 7 p.m.

Drive about 15 minutes from Fayetteville to Johnson, Arkansas, for sophisticated food in an airy setting at **James at the Mill** (3906 Greathouse Springs Road, Johnson; 479-443-1400; jamesatthemill.com;

$$-$$$$), on the grounds of the Inn at the Mill. The chef, Miles James, blends regional influences with contemporary cuisine, producing hybrid dishes like hickory-grilled pork tenderloin with goat cheese potato galette. The building, designed by the architect James Lambeth, is light-filled, elegant, and filled with interesting touches like the tall, varnished sycamore tree sunk in the bilevel dining room's foundation, its branches reaching to the ceiling.

SUNDAY

11 *Mountaineering* 11 a.m.
   Venture deeper into the Ozarks with a drive out of town. Spooky sandstone caves are open for exploring at **Devil's Den State Park** (Route 170, West Fork; 479-761-3325; mountainstateparks.com/devils-den), 25 miles south of Fayetteville. Or drive out on Routes 412 and 21 to the Ozark National Forest (fs.usda.gov/osfnf), where scenic trails reach forests, lakes, caves, and unusual rock formations.

ABOVE The Heartwood Gallery, a collective where Ozark artists sell their work.

THE BASICS

Northwest Arkansas Regional Airport is about 30 minutes from downtown Fayetteville. For the best experience, rent a car to get around.

Inn at Carnall Hall
465 North Arkansas Avenue
479-582-0402
innatcarnallhall.com
$$-$$$
A rosy brick Colonial Revival structure on the University of Arkansas campus, built in 1905 as a women's dormitory.

Dickson Street Inn
301 West Dickson Street
479-695-2100
dicksonstreetinn.com
$$
Boutique hotel in two Victorian buildings.

Inn at the Mill
3906 Greathouse Springs Road, Johnson
479-443-1800
innatthemill.com
$$
Built by the architect James Lambeth in and around a 19th-century gristmill.

Reynolds Razorback Stadium
Inn at Carnall Hall
W. MAPLE ST.
E. MAPLE ST.
N. ARKANSAS AVE.
W. LAFAYETTE ST.
N. COLLEGE AVE.
N. RAZORBACK RD.
UNIVERSITY OF ARKANSAS
Dickson Street Inn
3 GoodFolk Productions
E. DICKSON ST.
W. DICKSON ST.
1
N. SCHOOL AVE.
N. CHURCH AVE.
N. BLOCK AVE.
N. EAST AVE.
George's Majestic Lounge
W. FAIRVIEW ST.
CENTER ST.
Clinton House Museum **5**
Hugo's **2**
Town square/ Farmers' market **4**
S. CALIFORNIA BLVD.
Fayetteville Public Library **8**
W. MOUNTAIN ST.
E. ROCK ST.
Fayetteville
Heartwood Gallery **7**
E. SOUTH ST. **6**
Confederate cemetery **9**
S. SCHOOL AVE.
S. GOVERNMENT AVE.
Penguin Ed's B&B Bar-B-Q
E. SIXTH ST.
MILL DISTRICT
James at the Mill/ Inn at the Mill **10**
Johnson
GREATHOUSE SPRINGS RD.
265
1/4 MILE
45
ARKANSAS
Area of detail
540
16
62
3 MILES
71
11 To Devil's Den State Park

MISSOURI
Fayetteville
OZARK NATIONAL FOREST
TENN.
OKLA.
Arkansas R.
Little Rock
ARKANSAS
Mississippi R.
TEXAS LOUISIANA
MISS.

Oklahoma City

It shouldn't take more than a day for the song—who doesn't know that song?—to clear your head. Yes, a constant wind does seem to come sweepin' down the plain (more accurately, the red-dirt prairie). But amid the grand urban projects, gleaming museums, and air of new sophistication in today's Oklahoma City, the only folks yelling "Ayipioeeay" are likely to be visitors. Hints of what's behind the revitalization pop up everywhere: oil rigs, even on the State Capitol grounds. Even so, newcomers to town might wonder at first where they are. A generally flat cityscape, friendly hellos, and Chicago-style downtown architecture suggest the Midwest. Jazz, blues bars, and barbecue joints speak of the South. But the wide vistas and the American Indian shops (Oklahoma has 38 sovereign tribes), pickups, and cowboy hats tell another story: this is the West.
— BY FINN-OLAF JONES

FRIDAY

1 *Bricks and Bronzes* 4 p.m.

The Oklahoma River waterfront has come alive since 1999, when a canal was completed to attract visitors. In the lively Bricktown district, old ware-houses now hold restaurants, clubs, and shops. Catch the bold spirit by checking out the monumental commemoration of the great Land Run of 1889, when 10,000 people rushed into town on a single day. A series of bronze statues, the larger-than-life-size work of the sculptor Paul Moore, show pioneers, horses, and wagons charging into the fray. Nearby, duck inside for a look at some of the 300 banjos in the **American Banjo Museum** (9 East Sheridan Avenue; 405-604-2793; americanbanjomuseum.com), ranging from lavishly decorated Jazz Age beauties to replicas of slaves' homemade instruments.

2 *Wasabi on the Range* 7 p.m.

If you're in the mood for steak, you will never have far to look in Oklahoma City. But even if you're not, have dinner at the **Mantel Wine Bar & Bistro** (201 East

OPPOSITE Taxi boats on the canal in Bricktown, a happening Oklahoma City neighborhood.

RIGHT Oil has been good to Oklahoma, and derricks appear all over town, even on the grounds of the State Capitol.

Sheridan Avenue; 405-236-8040; themantelokc.com; $$). The menu honors the regional theme with several beef entrees, but also offers interesting alternatives like duck breast with cranberry port wine sauce or wasabi-encrusted tuna.

3 *You'll Never Bowl Alone* 9 p.m.

Check out the night life in Bricktown, where taxi boats ferry merrymakers to the teeming homegrown jazz and blues joints. One of the livelier spots is **RedPin** (200 South Oklahoma Avenue; 405-702-8880; bowlredpin.com), a 10-lane bowling alley masquer-ading as a nightclub. Rent some hip-looking high-top bowling shoes, grab a beer or a pomegranate martini, and bowl the night away.

SATURDAY

4 *Feed Your Inner Cowboy* 11 a.m.

South of the river, the century-old Oklahoma National Stockyards are still used for enormous cattle auctions several times a week, but there's another kind of show one block farther up at **Cattlemen's Steakhouse** (1309 South Agnew Avenue; 405-236-0416; cattlemensrestaurant.com; $$). Long lines form for lunch and dinner (no reservations taken), so try breakfast. "Usually it's just the old-timers that want this," a waitress said when one

out-of-towner succumbed to curiosity and ordered the calf brains. For the record, it looks like oatmeal, has a slight livery aftertaste, and isn't half bad. But wash it down with a couple of mugs of hot coffee and a plate of eggs and magnificently aged and tenderized steak.

5 *Dress Your Inner Cowboy* 12:30 p.m.

Cross the street to **Langston's Western Wear** (2224 Exchange Avenue; 405-235-9536; langstons.com) for your dungarees and boots, and then wander into the **National Saddlery Company** (1400 South Agnew Avenue; 405-239-2104; nationalsaddlery.com) for a hand-tooled saddle — prices run from about $1,500 for a base model to $30,000 for a masterpiece with silver trimmings. Down the street, **Shorty's Caboy Hattery** (1206 South Agnew Avenue; 405-232-4287; shortyshattery.com) will supply you with a custom-made cattleman's hat described by Mike Nunn, who manned the counter one day, as "the only hat that will stay on your head in Oklahoma wind." On the next block, **Oklahoma Native Art and Jewelry** (1316 South Agnew Avenue; 405-604-9800) carries a broad variety of items from Oklahoma's tribes. White pottery pieces with horse hairs burned onto their surfaces in Jackson Pollock-like swirling patterns are

ABOVE The memorial to victims of the 1995 bombing.

made by the store's owner, Yolanda White Antelope. Her son, Mario Badillo, creates silver jewelry.

6 *Where the West Is Found* 2 p.m.

James Earle Fraser's famous 18-foot statue of an American Indian slumped on his horse, *The End of the Trail*, greets you in the lobby of the **National Cowboy and Western Heritage Museum** (1700 Northeast 63rd Street; 405-478-2250; nationalcowboymuseum.org). Beware. You may think you can cover it in a couple of hours, but a whole day could be too little to reach the end of this trail. Exhibits in tentlike pavilions around a central courtyard cover everything about cowboys from their roots in Africa and England to how they operate on contemporary corporate ranches. Examine a replica of a turn-of-the-century cattle town; guns including John Wayne's impressive personal arsenal; and Western art including works by Frederic Remington, Albert Bierstadt, and Charles M. Russell.

7 *Cosmopolitans* 7 p.m.

The city's new economy has attracted a whole new class of settler, business types from world financial capitals, usually male and accompanied by stylish spouses. Find them — and a pre-dinner cocktail — in the noirish-cool **Lobby Bar** (4322 North Western Avenue; 405-604-4650; willrogerslobbybar.com) in the newly renovated Will Rogers Theater, which looms over an affluent corridor of North Western

Avenue. The street continues up to Tara-sized mansions dotting Nichols Hills, on the way passing establishments like **French Cowgirl** (4514 North Western Avenue; 405-604-4696), which sells tooled cellphone holders to match your saddle. For dinner, drive a few blocks to the **Coach House** (6437 Avondale Drive; 405-842-1000; thecoachhouseokc.com; $$-$$$), where the name of many an entree includes words borrowed from the French.

8 *Dances With Bulls* 10 p.m.

Find friends fast at **Cowboys OKC**, formerly Club Rodeo (2301 South Meridian Avenue; 405-686-1191; cowboysokc.com). Modern cowgirls and cowboys of every age group and shape can be found hootin' and hollerin' at this acre-sized honky-tonk south of downtown near the airport. Fellow carousers will help you figure out the dance moves to go with country sounds. The mood may turn real cowpokey when dance-floor lights go dark to be replaced by spotlights on a tennis-court-sized rodeo ring, where revelers migrate with their beers to watch hopefuls try to hang onto bucking bulls for longer than eight

ABOVE Shorty's Caboy Hattery. The cattleman's hat, they'll tell you at Shorty's, is the only kind that will stay on your head in an Oklahoma wind.

BELOW Downtown Oklahoma City.

that now covers the site, a gently flowing reflecting pool and two massive gates preside over 168 empty bronze chairs—one for each victim, the 19 smaller ones denoting children. Absorb the quiet, and the message.

10 *Under Glass* 11 a.m.

The **Oklahoma City Museum of Art** (415 Couch Drive; 405-236-3100; okcmoa.com) boasts the world's most comprehensive collection of glass sculptures by Dale Chihuly, starting with the 55-foot-tall centerpiece at the front door. Savor the mesmerizing play of light, color, and fantastic shapes, a fitting goodbye to a town that never seems shy about grabbing your attention.

ABOVE Sunset over the Oklahoma River.

OPPOSITE *The End of the Trail*, by James Earle Fraser, at the National Cowboy and Western Heritage Museum.

seconds. The loudest cheers have been known to go to the orneriest bulls.

SUNDAY

9 *The Memorial* 10 a.m.

All longtime residents of Oklahoma City seem to know exactly where they were at 9:02 a.m. on April 19, 1995, when Timothy McVeigh detonated an explosives-filled truck beneath the Alfred P. Murrah Federal Building, killing 168 people and damaging 312 surrounding buildings. At the **Oklahoma City National Memorial** (620 North Harvey Avenue; 405-235-3313; oklahomacitynationalmemorial.org)

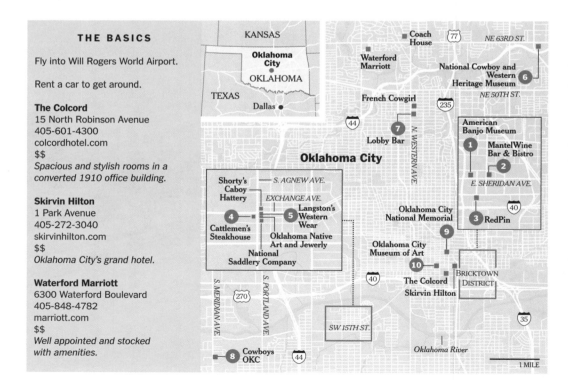

THE BASICS

Fly into Will Rogers World Airport.

Rent a car to get around.

The Colcord
15 North Robinson Avenue
405-601-4300
colcordhotel.com
$$
Spacious and stylish rooms in a converted 1910 office building.

Skirvin Hilton
1 Park Avenue
405-272-3040
skirvinhilton.com
$$
Oklahoma City's grand hotel.

Waterford Marriott
6300 Waterford Boulevard
405-848-4782
marriott.com
$$
Well appointed and stocked with amenities.

Kansas City

Kansas City, Missouri, is known for its barbecue, bebop, and easy-does-it Midwestern charm. Still a jazz mecca, the place where Charlie Parker, Lester Young, and Count Basie all got their start, it also has a newer and broader cultural richness. A decade-long effort to revitalize the downtown includes construction of the Kauffman Center for the Performing Arts, giving a sleek new home to the symphony, opera, and ballet. Yet while this metropolis on the Missouri River is no backwater, don't expect high polish. The city's best asset may be the unvarnished grit traceable all the way back to its days as the jumping-off point to the West on the Santa Fe Trail. — BY CHARLY WILDER

FRIDAY

1 *Crossroads Redefined* 4 p.m.

Industrial stagnation and suburban exodus in the 1960s left the Crossroads neighborhood nearly deserted. But now it is the **Crossroads Arts District** (kccrossroads.org), home to fashionable lofts in buildings like the former Western Auto offices, and to some 70 galleries. Two pioneering mainstays are **Sherry Leedy Contemporary Art** (2004 Baltimore Avenue; 816-221-2626; sherryleedy.com), which specializes in midcareer artists like Jun Kaneko, and the **Byron C. Cohen Gallery** (2020 Baltimore Avenue, Suite 1N; 816-421-5665; byroncohengallery.com), representing several artists from China. If it's the first Friday of the month, many galleries hold open houses until about 9 p.m.

2 *Sauce It Up* 7 p.m.

Debates over the best barbecue rouse as much passion here as religion or politics. Some swear by the old guard like Gates Bar-B-Q (gatesbbq.com) and Arthur Bryant's (arthurbryantsbbq.com), both of which have multiple branches. Others make the quick trip across the state line into Kansas City, Kansas, to a relative newcomer, **Oklahoma Joe's** (3002 West 47th Avenue; 913-722-3366; oklahomajoesbbq.com; $). It serves up pulled pork and beef brisket piled high on white bread, in a sauce that may just be the perfect amalgam of sweet, smoke, and vinegar.

OPPOSITE Kansas City's Crossroads district.

3 *Indie Scene* 11 p.m.

If the city's indie music scene hasn't garnered the same hype as those in other Midwestern cities like Minneapolis or Omaha, it's not for lack of guts or artistry. Homegrown bands like Ssion, a gender-bending art-punk music collective that has built a following with over-the-top live shows, cut their teeth in downtown galleries and dives. Hear up-and-comers at the **Record Bar** (1020 Westport Road; 816-753-5207; therecordbar.com) and the **Brick** (1727 McGee Street; 816-421-1634; thebrickkcmo.com). One of the newer spots is the **Czar Bar** (1531 Grand Boulevard; 816-221-2244; czarbar.com), owned by John Hulston, who also runs Anodyne Records, which counts the Meat Puppets, the BellRays, and Architects among its better-known acts.

SATURDAY

4 *Park Life* 10 a.m.

Kansas City is said to have more fountains than any other city except Rome. (This is difficult to prove, but with about 200 of them, it certainly has a good claim.) One of the loveliest can be found at **Jacob L. Loose Park** (51st Street and Wornall Road), a Civil War site, where the Laura Conyers Smith Fountain, made of Italian stone, is encircled by thousands of roses in some 150 varieties. The park is popular with picnicking families and bongo-playing teenagers on furlough from the suburbs.

5 *Contemporary Greens* Noon

If last night's barbecue has you yearning for a salad, head to **Café Sebastienne**, an airy, glass-covered restaurant at the **Kemper Museum of Contemporary Art** (4420 Warwick Boulevard; 816-561-7740; kemperart.org/cafe; $$). Seasonal greens come with cucumber, red onion, grape tomatoes, sheep's milk cheese, and grilled pita. After lunch, pop inside for a quick look at the Kemper's small but diverse collection of modern and contemporary works by artists like Dale Chihuly and Louise Bourgeois, whose gigantic iron spider sculpture looms over the front lawn.

6 *Art in a Cube* 1:30 p.m.

In 2007, the **Nelson-Atkins Museum of Art** (4525 Oak Street; 816-751-1278; nelson-atkins.org)

was thrust into the national spotlight when it opened a new wing designed by Steven Holl. The Bloch Building — which holds contemporary art, photography, and special exhibitions — consists of five translucent glass blocks that create what Nicolai Ouroussoff, the architecture critic of *The New York Times*, described as "a work of haunting power." The museum's suite of American Indian galleries shows an assemblage of about 200 works from more than 68 tribes.

7 *18th Street Couture* 4 p.m.

The Crossroads cultural awakening extends beyond art and into fashion. Three boutiques carrying the work of up-and-coming designers occupy a former film storage unit on West 18th Street. Peregrine Honig and Danielle Meister hand-pick lingerie and swimwear to carry at their shop, **Birdies** (116 West 18th Street; 816-842-2473; birdiespanties.com). Kelly Allen selects a quirky cross-section of locally designed clothing and accessories at **Spool** (122 West 18th Street; 816-842-0228). And **Peggy Noland** (124 West 18th Street; 816-221-7652; peggynoland.com) sells creations on the border of art and fashion in a shop that has often changed decor, at one time resembling the interior of a cloud, at another covered floor-to-ceiling with stuffed animals.

8 *Midwest Tapas* 7 p.m.

Stay in the Crossroads to sample modern Mediterranean-style tapas at **Extra Virgin** (1900 Main Street; 816-842-2205; extravirginkc.com; $$-$$$),

whose chef and owner is Kansas City's culinary titan, Michael Smith. The fare is more playful and adventurous than in his formal restaurant (called simply Michael Smith) next door. And if the loud, euro-chic décor, replete with a floor-to-ceiling *La Dolce Vita* mural, seems to be trying a little too hard, the crowd of unbuttoned professionals enjoying inspired dishes like crispy pork belly with green romesco and chick pea fries doesn't seem to mind. The menu is diverse, as is the wine list.

9 *'Round Midnight* 10 p.m.

The flashy new **Kansas City Power and Light District** (1100 Walnut Street; 816-842-1045; powerandlightdistrict.com) offers a wide range of bars, restaurants, and clubs that can feel like an open-air fraternity party. A smarter alternative can be found in the West Bottoms, an industrial neighborhood that draws a more urbane crowd. The **R Bar** (1617 Genessee Street; 816-471-1777; rbarkc.com) features live jazz and bluegrass, as well as old-time cocktails like Moscow mules and mint juleps. When midnight strikes, head to the **Mutual Musicians Foundation** (1823 Highland Avenue; 816-471-5212; thefoundationjamson.org). The legendary haunt opened in 1917, and public jam sessions are held every Saturday until around 6 a.m. For a small cover, you can catch impromptu sets by some of the city's undiscovered musicians in the same room where Charlie Parker had a cymbal thrown at him in 1937.

SUNDAY

10 *Viva Brunch* 10 a.m.

As any resident will tell you, Mexican food is a big deal here. One of the most authentic spots is **Ortega's**

ABOVE The Bloch Building, designed by Steven Holl, at the Nelson-Atkins Museum of Art.

Restaurant (2646 Belleview Avenue; 816-531-5415; ortegas.synthasite.com; $), tucked in the back of a mom-and-pop grocery store in midtown. On Sundays, its huevos rancheros draws a lively mix of churchgoing families and hung-over art students.

11 *Homage to the Greats* 11 a.m.
The **American Jazz Museum** and **Negro Leagues Baseball Museum** (1616 East 18th Street; 816-474-8463 and 816-221-1920; americanjazzmuseum.com and nlbm.com) share a building in the 18th and Vine Historic District, once the heart of the city's African-American shopping area. The jazz museum, with listening stations to bring the music to life, pays tribute to legendary jazz stars including Charlie

Parker, Louis Armstrong, Duke Ellington, and Ella Fitzgerald. The baseball museum is dedicated to the leagues where black stars like Satchel Paige, Josh Gibson, and Kansas City's own Buck O'Neil played until the integration of Major League Baseball in 1947. It was in Kansas City in 1920 that the first of them, the National Negro League, was founded.

ABOVE Sunday morning at Ortega's Restaurant.

THE BASICS

Several airlines serve Kansas City.

In town, you will want a car.

The Raphael
325 Ward Parkway
816-756-3800
raphaelkc.com
$$
Recently renovated bargain, with black marble bathrooms and flat-screen televisions.

Q Hotel + Spa
560 Westport Road
816-931-0001
theqhotel.com
$$
Eco-conscious hotel in the historic Westport district.

Hilton President Kansas City
1329 Baltimore Avenue
816-221-9490
hilton.com
$$
Downtown landmark built in 1926, redone in 2005.

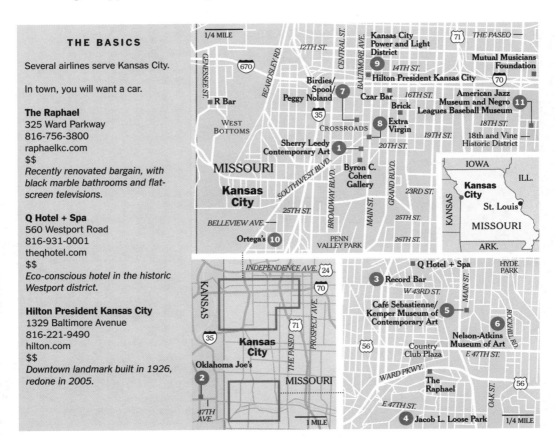

The Niobrara River Valley

To the uninitiated, Nebraska conjures a certain image: a treeless prairie steamrolled pancake-flat, stretching to the horizon. But tucked in a north-central patch of the state is the Niobrara River Valley, filled with a surprising collection of conifers and hardwoods, 200-foot sandstone bluffs, and spring-fed waterfalls. The Niobrara starts in eastern Wyoming and flows across Nebraska for more than 400 miles, emptying into the Missouri River. Seventy-six miles, starting just east of Valentine, are designated as national scenic river (nps.gov/niob). The rapids are mostly riffles, and the water is knee-deep in most spots, inviting a journey by canoe. And although a good float on the river is the center of your trip, there is more to see on land nearby. — BY HELEN OLSSON

FRIDAY

1 *Spurs and Saddles* 2 p.m.

In Valentine (population 2,820), red hearts are painted on the sidewalks and ranchers in cowboy hats roll down Main Street in dusty pickups. Browse the jeans, chaps, hats, ropes, and saddles at **Young's Western Wear** (143 North Main Street; 402-376-1281), purveyor of all things cowboy. Young's also stocks 5,000 pairs of cowboy boots, in snakeskin, elephant, stingray, ostrich, and — if you must — cow leather. Take time to stop by your float trip outfitter to make sure your reservations are in order for tomorrow. A handful of outfitters in Valentine rent canoes, kayaks, and giant inner tubes and can shuttle you or your car from point to point. One is **Little Outlaw** (1005 East Highway 20; 800-238-1867; outlawcanoe.com). If you canoe or kayak, you can run 22 miles from the Fort Niobrara Refuge to Rocky Ford in a day. A lazy float in a tube takes twice as long, so tubers might get only as far as Smith Falls by day's end.

2 *Under the Waterfall* 3:30 p.m.

Drive 23 miles south on Highway 97 through the Sandhills, past grazing cattle, massive spools of rolled hay, and spinning windmills, to **Snake River Falls**. (This Snake River is a tributary of the Niobrara.) Descend the trail through sumac and yucca to the base and crawl behind the 54-foot-wide falls to marvel at the gushing torrent inches away. Look for the cliff swallows' mud nests clinging to the limestone cliffs around the falls.

3 *Caribbean Meets Prairie* 5:30 p.m.

Three miles down Highway 97 is **Merritt Reservoir** (402-376-2969; outdoornebraska.ne.gov/parks.asp), a deep emerald lake rimmed by white sand beaches. Bury your toes in the warm sugar sand and look for the tiny tracks of sand toads. Anglers pull walleyes, crappies, and wide-mouth bass from the depths, and jet skiers trace arcs on the surface. When you're ready for dinner, find your way to the **Merritt Trading Post and Resort** (merritttradingpost.com), the only development at the lake, and its **Waters Edge** restaurant (402-376-1878; $$). Or stop for beef tenderloin or fresh walleye at the **Prairie Club** (402-376-1361; theprairieclub.com), a swanky golf course and country club that opened in 2010. It's 15 miles north of the reservoir on Highway 97.

4 *Yes, It's the Milky Way* 9 p.m.

Because of its remote location, the **Merritt Reservoir** is a prime spot for stargazing. "On a clear

OPPOSITE Floating on the Niobrara near Valentine, Nebraska. The river flows through Nebraska for 400 miles.

RIGHT An elk in the Valentine National Wildlife Refuge, in the Nebraska Sandhills.

moonless night, no kidding, it's so bright the Milky Way casts a shadow," said John Bauer, owner of the Merritt Trading Post and Resort. In late July or early August, amateur astronomers gather here for the annual Nebraska Star Party. They camp on the beach and crane their necks staring into the cosmos. If you're camping at the reservoir, you can gaze until sunrise. Otherwise, get back on the road by 10 or so and let the stars light your way back to Valentine.

SATURDAY

5 *Downriver with a Paddle* 9 a.m.
Grab sandwiches from Henderson's IGA or Scotty's Ranchland, Valentine's local grocers. (There's also a Subway in town.) Meet your outfitter at Cornell Bridge in the **Fort Niobrara National Wildlife Refuge**. Whatever your craft of choice — canoe, kayak, or inner tube — this is where you'll put in and float away on the shallow Niobrara. Over the eons, the Niobrara (pronounced nigh-oh-BRAH-rah) has cut more than 400 feet through a series of rock formations, pinkish-red, chalky white, and gray. Drifting in it is not unlike floating through an enormous block of Neopolitan ice cream. Beach your craft whenever you like and go for a swim or take a walk on shore. On the banks, wade through cold streams and search for small waterfalls tucked in side canyons. A recent National Park Service study found more than 230 falls, most only a few feet

high, tumbling into the river along a 35-mile stretch in this part of the Niobrara.

6 *In the Mist* Noon
Twelve miles down river, just past Allen Bridge, watch for signs along the riverbank for **Smith Falls State Park**. Stop to eat the picnic lunch you packed this morning. Stretch your legs with a short hike to the Smith Falls, Nebraska's tallest. Follow the trail across the steel truss Verdigre Bridge and up a winding boardwalk to the falls, where water plunges 63 feet over a bell-shaped rock. Surrounded by moss and mist, red cedar and bur oak, you'd be surprised to find that just a quick hike will take you to the dry, windswept Sandhills Prairie. The cool, moist environment in the river valley not only nurtures these familiar trees, but has preserved ancient species, like the giant paper birch that died out in the rest of Nebraska as the climate grew hotter and drier thousands of years ago. Animal life thrives here too: turkey vultures ride the thermals, sandpipers perch on sandbars, dragonflies dart above the water's surface.

ABOVE Stars, trailing across the sky in a time-lapse photograph, at the Merritt Reservoir, a lake south of Valentine. The remote reservoir is a prime stargazing spot.

OPPOSITE Sunset at the Merritt Reservoir.

7 *Floating Party Zone* 1:30 p.m.

By now, you are probably passing flotillas of summertime tubers from Iowa, Missouri, Kansas, and Nebraska — young things in bikinis and shorts, broiling in the sun and imbibing mightily. As bald eagles soar overhead, hip-hop may be thumping from boom boxes. Stuart Schneider, a park ranger, patrolled the river one late summer day, passing out mesh bags for empties. "On a busy Saturday, we can get 3,000 people," he said. "My favorite time on the river is the fall," he added. "The water is clear, there are no bugs, and the leaves can be spectacular." And, of course, the students will be back in school.

8 *Time to Take Out* 4:30 p.m.

Having paddled 22 miles, you can take out at **Rocky Ford**, where your outfitter will retrieve you and your canoe and shuttle you back to your car. Beyond Rocky Ford, there are Class III and IV rapids. Unless you have a death wish, exit here.

9 *Meat Eater's Paradise* 7 p.m.

Back in Valentine, reward yourself with a big aged Nebraska steak at **Jordan's** (404 East Highway 20; 402-376-1255). You're in cattle country after all. (Thursdays are livestock auction day in Valentine, where the buyers sit 10 deep on bleachers.) Of course, there isn't a menu in town that doesn't have chicken-fried steak. Jordan's is no exception.

SUNDAY

10 *Fuel Up* 10 a.m.

Have breakfast in Valentine at the **Bunkhouse Restaurant & Saloon** (109 East Highway 20; 402-376-1609; $). Under various names and owners, the Bunkhouse building has been serving grub since the 1940s. Slide into a booth and load up with a sirloin steak and eggs (when in Rome, you know…) or a stack of Joe's pancakes. Try a side order of Indian fry bread with powdered sugar or honey.

Rest assured the window you gaze out won't have the unseemly imprint of Valentine's infamous "Butt Bandit." The man who, for more than a year, left greasy prints of his nether regions on the windows of Valentine businesses was arrested in 2008.

11 *Birder's Paradise* 11 a.m.

Twenty miles south of Valentine, you'll find the **Valentine National Wildlife Refuge** (fws.gov/valentine). Where the Ogallala Aquifer nears the surface, bright blue lakes and marshes sparkle like jewels in the green grass. Hundreds of bird species

have been sighted here: sharp-tailed grouse, blue-winged teal, long-billed curlews. Just beyond the park's main headquarters, a trail mowed through the grass rises up to a rusting fire tower. From that perch, gaze at the Sandhills, which spread out like a turbulent sea in a hundred shades of green, blue and gold. It's time to reflect that the only pancake you've seen in Nebraska came with syrup and a generous pat of butter.

ABOVE A view of West Long Lake in the Valentine National Wildlife Refuge.

OPPOSITE Snake River Falls near the Merritt Reservoir. The rolling hills and waterfalls of the Niobrara Valley and land nearby are a surprise to outsiders who imagine Nebraska as filled with flat prairies.

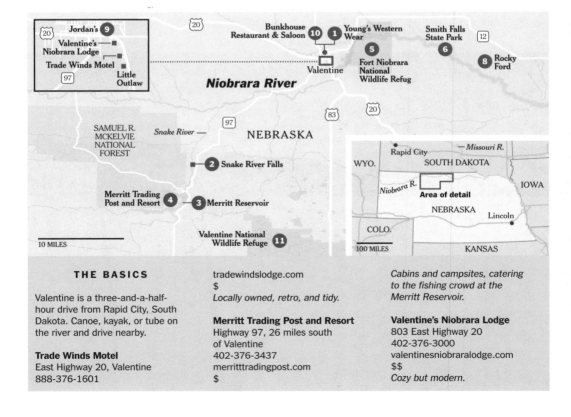

THE BASICS

Valentine is a three-and-a-half-hour drive from Rapid City, South Dakota. Canoe, kayak, or tube on the river and drive nearby.

Trade Winds Motel
East Highway 20, Valentine
888-376-1601

tradewindslodge.com
$
Locally owned, retro, and tidy.

Merritt Trading Post and Resort
Highway 97, 26 miles south of Valentine
402-376-3437
merritttradingpost.com
$

Cabins and campsites, catering to the fishing crowd at the Merritt Reservoir.

Valentine's Niobrara Lodge
803 East Highway 20
402-376-3000
valentinesniobraralodge.com
$$
Cozy but modern.

The Black Hills

Everything may, as they say, be big in Texas, but everything is positively monumental in the southwest corner of South Dakota, in and around the Black Hills. The caves are unusually cavernous, the badlands especially bad; the archaeological sites turn up mammoths. Giant faces gaze from more than one mountain. Drive through this sometimes hilly, sometimes flat, sometimes grassy, sometimes downright lunar landscape, and it will seem that every crossroad has a sign pointing to an outsize attraction, a national monument, or some other officially remembered site. — BY PAUL SCHNEIDER

FRIDAY

1 *Old Men of the Mountain* 3 p.m.

Begin at **Mount Rushmore National Memorial** (1300 Highway 244, Keystone; 605-574-3171; nps.gov/moru). Never mind that Teddy Roosevelt doesn't altogether fit in the group, or that the former republican solemnity of the place has been woefully squandered by the addition of imperial arches and

OPPOSITE The face of Crazy Horse, an Oglala Lakota chief, at the Crazy Horse Memorial, which has been gradually emerging from a granite mountain since 1948.

BELOW Sunset falls on Badlands National Park, an arid wilderness of singular beauty.

triumphal gewgaws at the entrance. And never mind if you are re-enacting a childhood visit to the place. A visit to Abe and the boys is a fitting start to your zigzagging tour through country where communal gawking and commemoration are de rigueur.

2 *Would Crazy Horse Approve?* 5 p.m.

Just outside Custer, appropriately, is the **Crazy Horse Memorial** (Avenue of the Chiefs, Crazy Horse; 605-673-4681; crazyhorsememorial.org), which when completed, its builders say, will be the largest sculpture on the planet. All of the presidential men on Rushmore would fit on the head of Crazy Horse, an Oglala Lakota chief, which has gradually been emerging from a granite mountain since 1948. The memorial already has what must be one of the world's largest interpretive centers, with all of the requisite snack and souvenir opportunities. The nonprofit, family-run place is somehow unnerving, as much a monument to monument makers and monument marketers as to the man who, with Sitting Bull, defeated George Armstrong Custer at the Little Bighorn. What Crazy Horse, who never permitted a photograph of himself to be taken, would have thought of laser shows projected on his graven image is anybody's guess, but Buffalo Bill Cody would have eaten it up.

3 *Comfort Food* 7 p.m.

Drive into the town of **Hot Springs** and take a quick walk around its eye-catching downtown of carved pink sandstone buildings. Yes, there really are hot springs here, once visited as healing waters and today marketed more as a theme park for children (evansplunge.com). Don't linger too long before finding your way to the **All Star Grill & Pub** (310 South Chicago Street; 605-745-7827; $) for burgers and hot roast beef sandwiches—restaurants close early out here.

SATURDAY

4 *Platters and Provisions* 8 a.m.

You're setting out for a long day of exploring, so have a hearty breakfast at **Dale's Family Restaurant** (745 Battle Mountain Avenue, Hot Springs; 605-745-3028; $), where you can expect hefty portions, standard eggs-and-bacon fare, and a cheerful local

crowd. Before leaving town, pick up some snacks and water. When hunger strikes again, you may be far from the nearest restaurant.

5 *Boys Will Be Boys* 9 a.m.

Even nature seems to be in the business of turning out stone memorials to fallen behemoths. On the southern outskirts of Hot Springs, a mass grave for mammoths is slowly emerging out of an ancient sink hole called the **Mammoth Site** (1800 U.S. 18 Bypass, Hot Springs; 605-745-6017; mammothsite.com). The effect is intensely sculptural: a mass of femurs and fibulas, skulls and tusks, backbones and pelvises, some just beginning to show in bas relief, some nearly freed from the surrounding matrix, some displayed behind glass. A few other animals have turned up in the hole, but it's mostly mammoths that ventured in and couldn't get out. And of those, nearly all seem to have been young males, the population most inclined, some mammoth experts have theorized, to risk-taking behavior.

6 *The Underground* 11 a.m.

Crystal lovers may prefer nearby Jewel Cave National Monument, which is one of the world's largest cavern systems, but **Wind Cave National Park** (nps.gov/wica; visitor center on Route 285 eleven miles north of Hot Springs) is only marginally less labyrinthine, with 134 miles of mapped passages. It is also where Crazy Horse and his fellow Lakota

believed a trickster spirit first convinced humans into coming above ground sometime back at the beginning of the world, which seems more in keeping with your monumental mission. Take along a jacket (it's chilly down there), and choose the tour that descends through the natural entrance rather than the elevator.

7 *Slow Roads* 2 p.m.

Take your time for an afternoon meander through some of the most beautiful parts of the Black Hills. Travel north on Route 87 through **Custer State Park** (custerstatepark.info) and turn right, toward Keystone, on Route 16A, which will take you through an improbable number of hairpin turns and one-lane tunnels in turreted mountains. For more of the same, check out the more crowded Route 87, the renowned **Needles Highway**. Either way, when you're ready to re-emerge, make your way north to Rapid City.

8 *Buffalo and a Nice Red* 8 p.m.

The **Corn Exchange** (727 Main Street, Rapid City; 605-343-5070; cornexchange.com; $$) has gained impressive national attention for its well-prepared food, which it describes as New Heartland Cuisine,

ABOVE Mount Rushmore National Memorial. The presidential heads are 60 feet high, with 20-foot noses.

and for its wine list. Relax over dinner (you should make a reservation) and scan the menu for the Buffalo Bolognese.

SUNDAY

9 *Not So Bad* 10 a.m.

The baddest parts of **Badlands National Park**—desiccated, vaguely Martian landscapes formed by erosion—aren't the whole story. Find an alternative on the **Sage Creek Rim Road** (in a convertible if you were smart enough to rent one), which overlooks rolling grasslands that stretch to the horizon. To get to it, leave I-90 at Exit 131, drive south on Route 240, which loops west just before the town called

Interior, and turn left at the sign a few miles past the Pinnacles Overlook. Stop at the Sage Creek primitive campground, where you can just walk off into the wide-open wilderness in whatever direction suits your fancy, following buffalo trails and creek beds.

10 *Quench It* 1 p.m.

Continue on the rim road to the intersection with Route 44 at the minuscule town of Scenic. Route 44 will take you scenically from here back to Rapid City, but stop in first at the **Old Longhorn Saloon** (101 Main Street, Scenic; 605-993-6133; $), the best place to get a cold beer in the middle of nowhere anywhere. Why should the folks with Harleys and halter tops have it all to themselves?

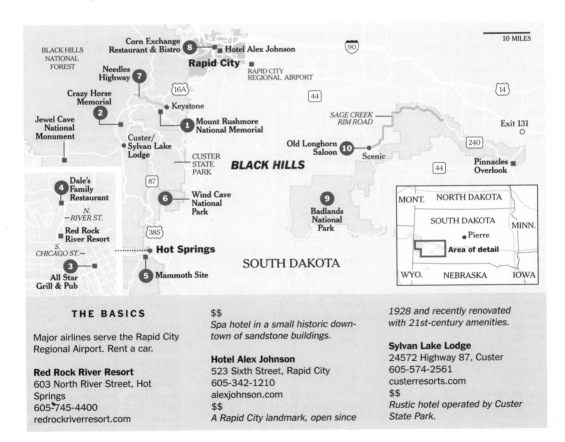

THE BASICS

Major airlines serve the Rapid City Regional Airport. Rent a car.

Red Rock River Resort
603 North River Street, Hot Springs
605-745-4400
redrockriverresort.com

$$
Spa hotel in a small historic downtown of sandstone buildings.

Hotel Alex Johnson
523 Sixth Street, Rapid City
605-342-1210
alexjohnson.com
$$
A Rapid City landmark, open since

1928 and recently renovated with 21st-century amenities.

Sylvan Lake Lodge
24572 Highway 87, Custer
605-574-2561
custerresorts.com
$$
Rustic hotel operated by Custer State Park.

Indexes

All images and text in this volume are © The New York Times unless otherwise noted. Any omissions for copy or credit are unintentional and appropriate credit will be given in future editions if such copyright holders contact the publisher.

Additional photo credits: Photo Courtesy of Arkansas Parks & Tourism, 102; Aurora Creative/ Getty Images, 2; Jumper/Getty Images, 52; Look/Getty Images, 21; Traverse City Convention & Visitors Bureau (www.traversecity.com), 44; Universal Images Group/Getty Images, 98; Jeremy Woodhouse/ Getty Images, 15.

Acknowledgments

We would like to thank everyone at *The New York Times* and at TASCHEN who contributed to the creation of this book.

For the book project itself, special recognition must go to Nina Wiener and Eric Schwartau at TASCHEN, the dedicated editor and assistant behind the scenes; to Natasha Perkel, the *Times* artist whose clear and elegantly crafted maps make the itineraries comprehensible; to Phyllis Collazo of the *Times* staff, whose photo editing gave the book its arresting images; and to Olimpia Zagnoli, whose illustrations and illustrated maps enliven every article and each regional introduction.

Guiding the deft and artful transformation of newspaper material to book form at TASCHEN were Marco Zivny, the book's designer; Josh Baker, the art director; and Jennifer Patrick, production manager. Also at TASCHEN, David Martinez, Jessica Sappenfeld, Anna-Tina Kessler, Kirstin Plate and Janet Kim provided production assistance, and at the *Times*, Heidi Giovine helped at critical moments. Craig B. Gaines copy-edited the manuscript.

But the indebtedness goes much further back. This book grew out of the work of all of the editors, writers, photographers, and *Times* staff people whose contributions and support for the weekly "36 Hours" column built a rich archive over many years.

For this legacy, credit must go first to Stuart Emmrich, who created the column in 2002 and then refined the concept and guided its development over eight years, first as the *Times* Escapes editor and then as Travel editor. Without his vision, there would be no "36 Hours."

Great thanks must go to all of the writers and photographers whose work appears in the book, both *Times* staffers and freelancers.

And a legion of *Times* editors behind the scenes made it all happen, and still do.

Danielle Mattoon, who took over as Travel editor in 2010, has brought her steady hand to "36 Hours," and found time to be supportive of this book as well.

Suzanne MacNeille, now the column's direct editor, and her predecessors Jeff Z. Klein and Denny Lee have all superbly filled the role of finding and working with writers, choosing and assigning destinations, and assuring that the weekly product would entertain and inform readers while upholding *Times* journalistic standards. The former Escapes editors Amy Virshup and Mervyn Rothstein saw the column through many of its early years, assuring its consistent quality.

The talented *Times* photo editors who have overseen images and directed the work of the column's photographers include Lonnie Schlein, Jessica DeWitt, Gina Privitere, Darcy Eveleigh, Laura O'Neill, Chris Jones, and the late John Forbes. The newspaper column's design is the work of the *Times* art director Rodrigo Honeywell.

Among the many editors on the *Times* Travel and Escapes copy desks who have kept "36 Hours" at its best over the years, three who stand out are Florence Stickney, Steve Bailey, and Carl Sommers. Editors of the column on the *New York Times* web site have been Alice Dubois, David Allan, Miki Meek, Allison Busacca, and Danielle Belopotosky. Much of the fact-checking, that most invaluable and unsung of skills, was in the hands of Rusha Haljuci, Nick Kaye, Anna Bahney, and George Gustines.

Finally, we must offer a special acknowledgment to Benedikt Taschen, whose longtime readership and interest in the "36 Hours" column led to the partnership of our two companies to produce this book.

— BARBARA IRELAND AND ALEX WARD

Copyright © 2013 *The New York Times*. All Rights Reserved.

Editor Barbara Ireland
Project management Alex Ward
Photo editor Phyllis Collazo
Maps Natasha Perkel
Spot illustrations and region maps Olimpia Zagnoli
Editorial coordination Nina Wiener and Eric Schwartau
Art direction Marco Zivny and Josh Baker
Layout and design Marco Zivny
Production Jennifer Patrick

To stay informed about upcoming TASCHEN titles, please request our magazine at www.taschen.com/magazine or write to TASCHEN, Hohenzollernring 53, D–50672 Cologne, Germany, contact@taschen.com. We will be happy to send you a free copy of our magazine which is filled with information about all of our books.

©2013 TASCHEN GmbH
Hohenzollernring 53, D–50672 Köln, www.taschen.com

ISBN 978-3-8365-4200-5 Printed in China

TRUST *THE NEW YORK TIMES* WITH YOUR NEXT 36 HOURS

"The ultimate weekend planner for the literate by the literate — where even Oklahoma City can be as alluring as Paris." —AMAZON READER REVIEW

AVAILABLE IN *THE NEW YORK TIMES* 36 HOURS SERIES

150 WEEKENDS IN THE USA & CANADA*

Weekends on the road. The ultimate travel guide to the USA and Canada

125 WEEKENDS IN EUROPE

(Re)discovering Europe: dream weekends with practical itineraries from Paris to Perm

* also available for iPad

USA & CANADA REGION BY REGION

NORTHEAST

SOUTHEAST

MIDWEST & GREAT LAKES

SOUTHWEST & ROCKY MOUNTAINS

WEST COAST

FOR NEWS ON UPCOMING BOOKS IN THIS SERIES, VISIT WWW.TASCHEN.COM

MIDWEST
& GREAT LAKES

Duluth
40

the Black Hills
122

MINNEAPOLIS
St. Paul 36

Madison 32

MILWAU

Oak Pa

the Niobrara
River Valley 116

Iowa's
Mississippi
river 92

Kansas
City 112

St. Louis 98

Fayetteville
102

Oklahoma City 106